W9-DDJ-221

THE UNITED NATIONS
A Concise History

By
Christopher D. O'Sullivan

AN ANVIL ORIGINAL
Under the general editorship of
Hans L. Trefousse

KRIEGER PUBLISHING COMPANY
MALABAR, FLORIDA
2005

Original Edition 2005

Printed and Published by
KRIEGER PUBLISHING COMPANY
KRIEGER DRIVE
MALABAR, FLORIDA 32950

Copyright © 2005 by Christopher D. O'Sullivan

All rights reserved. No part of this book may be reproduced in any form or by any
means, electronic or mechanical, including information storage and retrieval systems
without permission in writing from the publisher.
No liability is assumed with respect to the use of the information contained herein.
Printed in the United States of America.

FROM A DECLARATION OF PRINCIPLES JOINTLY ADOPTED BY A
COMMITTEE OF THE AMERICAN BAR ASSOCIATION AND A COM-
MITTEE OF PUBLISHERS:
This publication is designed to provide accurate and authoritative information in regard to the subject matter covered. It is sold with the understanding that the publisher
is not engaged in rendering legal, accounting, or other professional service. If legal
advice or other expert assistance is required, the services of a competent professional
person should be sought.

Library of Congress Cataloging-in-Publication Data

O'Sullivan, Christopher D.
  The United Nations : a concise history / by Christopher D. O'Sullivan.
    p. cm. — (The anvil series)
  Includes bibliographical references and index.
  ISBN 1-57524-223-0 (alk. paper)
    1. United Nations—History. I. Title. II. Anvil series (Huntington, N.Y.)

JZ4986.O88   2005
341.23′09—dc22   2004061610

10 9 8 7 6 5 4 3

THE ANVIL SERIES

Anvil paperbacks give an original analysis of a major field of history or a problem area, drawing upon the most recent research. They present a concise treatment and can act as supplementary material for college history courses. Written by many of the outstanding historians in the United States, the format is one-half narrative text, one-half supporting documents, often from hard to find sources.

CONTENTS

PART I—The United Nations: A Concise History

PART II—Documents

CONTENTS   vii

PART I

THE UNITED NATIONS:
A CONCISE HISTORY

INTRODUCTION

At first glance, a concise history of the United Nations sounds like a contradictory endeavor. The UN has been involved in almost every global issue and dispute during the past six decades. Selectivity is necessary, but it can be difficult. I have thus chosen six major themes for Part I: the inspirations and origins of the United Nations and early precedents; the United Nations and the Cold War; the emergence of the Third World and the debate over economic development and the global economy; the UN's role in the Middle East; the United Nations and Africa; and the challenges the UN has faced since the Cold War. Within these themes the reader will find much detail and many hotly contested debates. Part II features 31 primary source documents, ranging from the founding documents of the United Nations, significant Security Council and General Assembly Resolutions, official reports and studies, and tables and charts.

Chapter 1 explores the inspirations for the UN's predecessor organization, the League of Nations, and traces the origins of the United Nations from the League precedent, through the 1941 Atlantic Conference and 1944 Dumbarton Oaks Conference, to the San Francisco Conference of 1945 which created the UN Charter. It examines the structure of the United Nations, delineating the differences between the Security Council and the General Assembly. It also assesses the tenures of various Secretaries General, the role of the International Court of Justice, the International Monetary Fund, and the World Bank.

Chapter 2 focuses on the United Nations in the Cold War struggle that dominated relations among states during the UN's first four decades. The United Nations played a significant role in the Korean War (1950–1953), but it would be marginalized during the Soviet invasion of Hungary (1956), the Cuban Missile Crisis (1962), and the Vietnam War (c. 1964–1975). The controversy over seating the People's Republic of China on the Security Council and the growing antagonism between the United Nations and the United States over Cold War objectives—particularly in Central America—also preoccupied the United Nations during this time. The UN played a role in resolving the Soviet-Afghan conflict (1979–1989) and faced new challenges in the emerging post-Cold War world. This chapter also examines whether the United Nations helped check Cold War tensions, averting the kind of great power cataclysms that devastated so much of the world in the three previous decades. Did the UN system in fact allow the great powers to air their grievances and score political and rhetorical points without resort to war? Did it provide an institutional framework where crises and tensions could be addressed and communication maintained?

Chapter 3 explores the emergence of the Third World as a significant factor in the politics of the UN, as well as its impact on the international system. The nonaligned movement emerged in the 1950s and 1960s and inspired developing countries to create a Third World caucus—the group of 77—within the General Assembly. Debates raged at the United Nations in the 1960s and 1970s over trade and development and continue today over globalization. The UN has also worked to resolve a number of conflicts occurring within the developing world, such as the long-running India-Pakistan dispute and the crisis in East Timor.

The UN's role in the Middle East is discussed in Chapter 4, beginning with the effort to partition Palestine (1947–1948) and the ongoing Arab-Israeli dispute, the UN's role in various other Middle East crises including the war over Suez (1956), the several emergencies over Lebanon (1958, 1978–1990), and the civil war in Yemen (c.1962–1970). Chapter 4 also highlights the UN's role in the various Iraq crises: the first (1990–91) highlighted the potential of the Security Council in the post-Cold War context, whereas the second (2002–04) damaged the harmony of the council and led to a serious breach between Washington and the United Nations.

The UN has been very active in Africa. Chapter 5 begins with a historical analysis of why Africa presents the United Nations with so many challenges. The UN dispatched a large peacekeeping mission to the Congo in 1960–61 and has been involved in the more recent wars plaguing that nation and the broader Great Lakes region of Africa. The UN was involved from the very beginning with the efforts to end white rule in Rhodesia, South Africa, and Namibia; and it worked to mitigate the consequences of the Cold War in Mozambique and Angola. The UN's ill-fated efforts at nation building in Somalia (1993) would have profound consequences, not only for Somalia but also in discouraging any effort to halt the genocide in Rwanda (1994).

Chapter 6 examines the years after the Cold War and discusses the way in which the post-Cold War decade represented a lost opportunity for reordering world politics. The United Nations has faced numerous challenges in the post-Cold War era, including the expansion of peacekeeping and nation building, the upheavals associated with globalization, international terrorism, and human rights, as well as new challenges in world health.

I have sought to provide some historical background to the many controversies the United Nations has faced, rather than merely discuss conflicts as if they had no history or context, or occurred through spontaneous combustion. Not surprisingly, a large number of the conflicts the UN has sought to resolve have imperial and colonial origins, particularly those of the Middle East and Africa, but also many in south and east Asia and even Europe, the Caribbean, and Latin America. Understanding these colonial ramifications is essential to comprehending world politics today. Thus, one of the underlying themes of this book is decolonization and the impact it had on the international system during the history of the United Nations. The process of decolonization and its consequences features prominently in every chapter of this book.

CHAPTER 1

FROM THE LEAGUE OF NATIONS TO THE CREATION OF THE UNITED NATIONS

The League of Nations. Both the League of Nations and its successor, the United Nations, were born from the trauma of catastrophic world wars. Both began at a particular historical moment when, after intense human suffering, the world attempted to alter the course of history by pooling state sovereignty into a collective whole. The origins of both the League and the United Nations cannot be understood without emphasizing this historical context from which they evolved. Although the League's shortcomings and ultimate failure have often been the chief focus of many of those who have assessed it, it represented a remarkable experiment in transforming the relations among sovereign nation states. Never before in world history had so many nations come together voluntarily to radically reconfigure the international system. The League's ultimate collapse should not detract from the significance of that experiment.

The League is worth examining, if even briefly, because it served in many ways as the primary model for the United Nations. While they shared similar organizational architecture, there are also essential differences. Those who planned the United Nations had studied the structure and functions of the League, not only as a guidepost, but also in the hope of avoiding its problems. This effort to avoid the mistakes of the League would take the creators of the United Nations in a number of significantly new directions. It is thus worth examining the League in some detail, also recalling some of the intellectual and political inspirations that led to its creation, a number of them long preceding World War I. The League was very much a result of the horrors of the war of 1914–1918. Many feared that nation states would continue to utilize industrial technologies to kill and maim more efficiently than ever before. Civilization might not survive another such conflict. The Great War demonstrated that wars could not always be contained or limited, and that innovations in weaponry and national mobilization had given states immense power to wage war and to sustain devastating human and material losses. Yet the League was not merely a reaction to the carnage of the Great War. Humanity had been seeking peace for cen-

7

turies with little to show for its efforts. The emergence of numerous
nation-states, each pursuing its national aims at the expense of other
sovereign powers, had created a highly unstable international system
where war, if limited and brief, could serve as just another instrument
in the pursuit of national interests.

As modern nation-states began to emerge from the Middle Ages,
statesmen looked for innovative ways to promote stability in the international system. The seventeenth-century French statesman, the duc
de Sully (1560–1641), advocated a federation of all Christian nations
and, later, the eighteenth-century Prussian philosopher Immanuel Kant
(1724–1804) envisioned a voluntary federation of states to settle disputes and outlaw territorial acquisition by force. Just as with today's
contentious debate over the efficacy of international cooperation, for
every Sully or Kant there was also a Machiavelli, a Hobbes, or a Hegel,
championing unilateral state power and, with equal vigor, the notion
that the normal behavior of states was aggressive and aggrandizing.

In the century before the League, there were a number of important
steps toward international cooperation. The Congress of Vienna system,
coming after the turmoil of the Napoleonic era, sought to create a Con-
cert of Europe, established an important precedent: that nation-states
could work cooperatively if they perceived that cooperation was in their
interest. Other transnational efforts such as the establishment of an international postal union and the Red Cross, demonstrated the increasingly integrated nature of the modern era, as did the series of Geneva
Conventions establishing norms of behavior among nations. The century between the end of the Napoleonic wars in 1815 and the outbreak
of the Great War in 1914 was one of relative harmony among European
states, demonstrating that war and aggrandizement at the expense of
others were not the only legitimate pursuits of nations.

The more immediate inspiration for the League lay in the several
years preceding its birth. The horrific slaughter of the Great War provoked widespread revulsion and a strong desire to prevent a repetition.
The war also revealed the increasing instability of the international system. Nation-states, pursuing there own aims, had plunged the world
into a war that swept away the Russian, Austro–Hungarian, and Ottoman empires, resulted in the disappearance of the German imperial dynasty, and seriously undermined Britain and France as world powers.
Many came away from the war—a war that claimed the lives of tens of
millions—with a determination to fundamentally reform the interna-

tional order. As the war entered its last year in 1918, the American President Woodrow Wilson proclaimed his Fourteen Points, calling for a new diplomacy to replace the unstable international system. (*See Document No. 1.*) Included was a proposal for a League of Nations to promote collective security in the postwar era.

At the Paris Peace Conference the victorious powers not only discussed the disposition of peoples and territories but also worked to create a League of voluntarily participating nations. Not only did this mark an important development in the historical relations among states, it also represented a change in views toward sovereignty and the nation state, as well as support for the national self-determination of peoples. The creation of a League offered a powerful critique of the old thinking about world politics, further underscoring that the nation-state was in crisis and that the world might not recover from another world war. The fate of Russia, Germany, Austria-Hungary, and the Ottoman Empire certainly lent strength to that argument. Furthermore, because of its provisions for League mandates to be established over colonial territories lost by the defeated powers, the League also provided a kind of moral critique of colonialism. Wilsonian war aims, such as national self-determination, could not be trumpeted while the spoils of war were parceled out to the victors as in times past. Most of the powers engaged in the war—including the United States—had empires where millions of subject peoples languished without political or economic rights, or hope of progress of any sort. The mandates would—or at least were intended to—serve as means to protect such territories from further exploitation and, in some cases, prepare them for eventual self-rule.

As designed by the peacemakers at Paris (and, before them, by the American postwar planners known as Wilson's Inquiry) the structure of the League resembled that of the later United Nations. It would possess a council of four great powers—Britain, France, Italy, and Japan (the US was slated to be a permanent member but subsequently declined)—and an assembly of all members, 29 initially. Four members of the assembly would join the council on a rotating, nonpermanent, basis. Perhaps the most noteworthy innovation was that the League Covenant (*see Document No. 2*) granted the council the power to impose sanctions against states violating international norms. (*See Document No. 3.*)

The launching of the League in Geneva in 1920 was greeted with much optimism, yet there were problems from the outset. As noted, the decision by the United States, the largest of the victorious powers and the chief creator of the League, not to join delivered a blow to the League's prestige. Moreover, it handicapped future efforts to create a workable system of collective security. Another impediment was that both the newly established Soviet Union and Weimar Germany were not initially allowed in, although both eventually joined—Germany in 1926 and the USSR in 1934. The lack of concurrent membership of these powers put meaningful collective security out of reach. The League faced new challenges as the postwar era entered a period of renewed nationalism. There was, for example, growing power and assertiveness on the part of the so-called revisionist powers that were discontented with the Versailles system, such as Italy, Germany, and Japan. These problems were made more difficult by the flaws in the League's structure and functioning. For example, unanimity was required for all decisions in both the Council and the Assembly, leading to frequent paralysis.

Despite these handicaps, the League enjoyed a number of important achievements, which have often been overlooked by its critics. It established precedents for the use of plebiscites, mediation, conciliation, and fact-finding as legitimate tools for preserving peace and maintaining international harmony. It mediated Finnish-Swedish tensions over the disputed Aland Islands in 1921, pledged to guarantee the territorial integrity of a tiny Albania threatened by its neighbors, aided Austria with its postwar economic problems, settled the dispute between Germany and Poland over Upper Silesia in 1922, and it established rudimentary prototypes for peacekeeping in disputes in Vilna (1920) and the Saar (1934–35).

Uppermost in popular memory, however, are the areas where the League failed. It failed to resolve the Russo-Polish War of 1920–21. It passively allowed the French occupation of the Ruhr in 1923 and found it increasingly difficult to resist Italian encroachments in Albania throughout the late 1920s and 1930s. It did not respond effectively when Germany remilitarized the Rhineland in 1936, or when it annexed Austria in 1938. Furthermore, the League exerted little *de facto* control over the mandated territories, particularly Palestine, Lebanon, and Iraq. Throughout Africa, Britain and France continued unrestrained in their efforts to reconfigure—socially, politically, and economically—areas under their control. This would have profound consequences for the future of those territories. The problematic nature of the mandates aside, the peace settlement of 1919 had made a number of other matters worse, which further revealed the weakness of collective security in a world of sovereign states pursuing their own interests. Many of the new states created out of the wreckage of the German, Russian, and Austro-Hungarian empires in Europe were unstable, creating an environment where numerous states jockeyed to achieve their overlapping and competing national aims. As the Versailles system began to crumble in the 1930s, the League became increasingly weakened in its efforts to promote peace as it entered its second decade.

Italian premier Benito Mussolini's attack on Abyssinia in 1935 was a trauma to the League system from which it never fully recovered. Gambling that Italy could keep pace with the British and French empires, Mussolini—without provocation, in the absence of any valid justification, and in the face of opposition from other great powers—invaded Abyssinia in October. Had Mussolini done this in a previous era, before the creation of the League and the experiment with the mandates, the other great powers might have accommodated his objectives, even if after much diplomatic wrangling. But the League, despite its shortcomings, had changed the tenor of international politics. The old diplomacy was supposed to have gone out of fashion with the launching of the League, and Mussolini's actions were perceived as a serious threat to international order. Prior to Mussolini's invasion, Abyssinia, as a member of the League, had sought in Geneva to resolve its problems peacefully with Italy. The League recognized the strength of Abyssinia's case but ultimately failed to find some means of preventing an Italian invasion and eventual annexation.

Germany's withdrawal from the League in October 1933 and its unopposed occupation of the Rhineland in March 1936 further revealed the League's growing irrelevance in the increasingly aggressive climate of the 1930s. The League also failed to do anything about the Spanish Civil War (1936–1939), where the democratic government of Spain (also a member of the League) was attacked by its own military led by General Francisco Franco, who was supported by the Fascist regimes in Italy and Germany. This, coupled with Japan's earlier annexation of Manchuria (1931) and its wider war launched against China in July 1937, further contributed to the breakdown of the international system. With Germany's dismemberment of Czechoslovakia between 1938 and 1939, its attack on Poland in September 1939, the Soviet annexation of Eastern Poland and its later attack on Finland in November, and the subsequent expulsion of the USSR from the League in December, it had become obvious that the interwar international system, and the League of Nations with it, had completely disintegrated.

Judged by the goals enunciated by its founders, the League failed to measure up to much of its original promise and ultimately was unable to perform even its most basic functions. Yet, if one assesses the League experiment in the broader context of historical trends in the relations among states, it still stands as a remarkable innovation. It also established a number of important precedents that carried over into the era of the United Nations, such as the effort to promote collective security, and the trend away from unilateral great power politics toward more cooperative, consensual approaches to the problems of the world. Perhaps most important, the League structure itself served as a precedent for the next effort at creating an international organization.

Planning a New World Organization: From the Atlantic Charter to the San Francisco Conference. The outbreak of World War II exposed the failures of the interwar international system and the League. But the war inspired a rich debate about the way nation-states interacted with one another. In both Britain and the United States, officials began discussing the creation of a new international system. To many, the carnage of the two world wars demonstrated clearly that the great powers must establish a new order in relations among nations.

At the first wartime Roosevelt-Churchill summit meeting, known as the Atlantic Conference, off the coast of Newfoundland in August 1941, the two leaders issued a joint declaration known as the Atlantic Charter (*see Document No. 4*), which vaguely pledged the allies to create a "permanent system of general security." The US was still four months from entering the war and Roosevelt remained cautious about further arousing domestic opposition. But the Atlantic Charter encouraged those who sought to create a new world order with a new international organization as its centerpiece. Less than a month after Pearl Harbor, representatives of 26 nations gathered in Washington to sign a Declaration by the United Nations (*see Document No. 5*), the first time the term "United Nations" had been used. Perhaps of greater significance, Roosevelt simultaneously authorized the launching of an extensive program of postwar planning. Several advisory committees on the problems of the postwar world had been launched at the state department as early as 1939, suspended after the fall of France in 1940, and revived again after Pearl Harbor.

While Roosevelt remained supportive of many aspects of Wilsonianism, he believed much of the previous effort at postwar planning had been flawed. He aimed to avoid repeating mistakes such as the failure to create the League Covenant during the war and Wilson's refusal to involve Congress (particularly the opposition Republicans) in the planning process. He also sought to avoid the flaws of the mandates system. The very nature of this planning was a critique of both the League and Wilson's failed effort to secure American participation. The American postwar planners sought to avoid the problems of the League yet the League still stood as an important model. The Covenant of the League of Nations was used liberally as a rough blueprint.

Throughout the war, the US remained ahead of other powers in postwar planning. This was a distinctively American project. International institutions would be created with an eye to how they could best promote American aims and interests around the world. International economic institutions would be created to project American commercial interests on a global scale. Any new effort to create an international organization would have to reconcile American interests with international institutions. Anything less was seen as coming perilously close to repeating Wilson's errors. This time, an international organization would be more bluntly promoted as advancing American aims, interests, and values in the world. When British Foreign Secretary Anthony Eden visited Washington in March 1943, Roosevelt shared with him the American postwar planning proposals, startling the British into fits of activity. This first phase of US postwar planning concluded in July 1943 when the advisory committees submitted to the president detailed recommendations, including a completed blueprint for a new international organization. The planners felt that the League, despite its many failings, had established significant precedents for international cooperation. It marked a revolutionary advance over previous relationships among nation states, and should serve as a prototype for the new organization.

The Anglo-American Quebec Conference in August 1943 produced a draft declaration marking a general commitment on the part of Britain, the United States, China, and the Soviet Union to a new international organization. At Quebec, British and American officials agreed to seek Stalin's future approval for their postwar plans while the war still raged. At the subsequent Moscow Conference of October 1943, Secretary of State Cordell Hull brought with him a blueprint of American postwar plans. He sought to convince the Soviets that participation in an international organization could serve their own national interests. The Moscow Conference resulted in yet another declaration pledging support for an international organization.

During the subsequent Big Three summit in Teheran in December 1943, Roosevelt shared with Stalin the blueprint for an international organization worked out in Washington over the previous two years. At the Dumbarton Oaks Conference in Washington the four major allies, meeting in two sessions between August and October 1944, settled a number of disagreements, particularly over voting procedures. As Robert Hilderbrand has described in *Dumbarton Oaks: The Origins of the United Nations and the Search for Postwar Security,* unlike the League, the new world body would be created separate from the peace treaties. The resulting documents, the Dumbarton Oaks Proposals (*see Document No. 6*), owed much to the previous two years of American postwar planning, and would serve as the basis for the United Nations Charter. The proposals focused on a security council, an assembly, a world court, and a secretariat. Just prior to Dumbarton Oaks, a conference on creating a new international financial system, held at Bretton Woods, New Hampshire, established blueprints for creating international economic institutions as part of the United Nations system. It included the International Bank for Reconstruction and Development (the World Bank) (*see Document No. 7*) and the International Monetary Fund. (*See Document No. 8*)

After Dumbarton Oaks, a number of issues remained to be ironed out. Foremost was Roosevelt conceding to Stalin a Security Council veto at the February 1945 Yalta Conference. Roosevelt died in April 1945 and thus did not live to see the fruition of so much planning for world organization. But in that same month, in a remarkable demonstration of multilateral diplomacy, delegates representing 50 nations gathered from April to June 1945 in San Francisco and produced the Charter of the United Nations, containing 19 chapters and 111 articles and providing a framework for the UN's wide range of activities. (*See Document No. 9.*)

Launching the United Nations and Establishing Precedents. The Charter of the United Nations determines its structure in theory, but the first few years of the UN would establish a number of precedents determining how the institutions would work in practice, testing its institutional framework. No sooner had the United Nations been launched when it became apparent that its course would be profoundly affected by the accelerating Cold War. The global confrontation between the superpowers and their allies would paralyze the United Nations, particularly the Security Council, but would also inspire unanticipated innovations in the way the UN functions.

The Security Council. The Security Council arose from the precedent established by the council of the League of Nations. Today the Security Council has 15 members, five of whom—the United States, Britain, France, Russia, and China—have permanent status with veto power. The other 10 are elected to the Security Council by the General Assembly to two-year nonrenewable terms. The nonpermanent 10 are elected on a staggered basis, with five new members brought on board each year for two-year terms. Selection is based on geographical distribution, with five nonpermanent members from Africa and Asia, two from Latin America, two from Western Europe, and one from Eastern Europe. The number of nonpermanent members was increased from six to 10 in 1965.

The Security Council is the primary body for dealing with matters of war and peace, recommending to the General Assembly candidates for the post of Secretary General, recommending new member states to the General Assembly, and electing, in cooperation with the General Assembly, justices of the World Court. Over the years there have been frequent calls for reform of the Security Council and its procedures. The five permanent members were the principal world powers at the time of the drafting of the Charter and were the primary allies in World War II. The fairness of this has been debated, but any change in the composition of the Security Council requires an amendment to the UN Charter, and that requires the consent of all five permanent members. The Charter has only been amended five times since its drafting in 1945 and it is unlikely that any substantive structural changes will occur anytime soon.

The veto has remained one of the most controversial subjects in the UN's history, provoking much disagreement. It is increasingly seen as a means by the permanent five to stymie efforts at collective security but the great powers' reliance upon the veto—more than 250 have been cast so far—demonstrates how unlikely any reform of the process is. UN scholar Evan Luard has observed that the creators of the Charter assumed there would be numerous parts of the world the great powers would have no interest in, and therefore the veto would be employed only in matters of vital national interest. He has noted that this was quickly disproved with the globalization of the Cold War, because there was no part of the world, however remote, which ultimately was not regarded as essential to the interests of the great powers.

The General Assembly. The only United Nation body where all member states are equally represented with one vote, and the only truly global forum in the world, the General Assembly's powers at times overlap those of the other UN bodies. It has the power to discuss any issue brought before it, but its resolutions are non-binding. Its decisions on routine matters are determined by a simple majority of members voting, whereas a two-thirds majority is required for matters of greater importance, such as revision of the Charter or the admission of new members. An important development in the history of the General Assembly occurred in 1950 with the passage of the Uniting for Peace Resolution, which allowed for the calling of an emergency session when the Security Council is deadlocked. The General Assembly has often provided a locale for nations to conduct behind-the-scenes diplomacy and to establish informal contacts with other states and representatives of stateless peoples. In recent years, the issue of whether future membership should be restricted to nation-states, or expanded to include non-state representatives, has been debated.

The Secretariat and the Secretary General. Serving as the international civil service of the United Nations, the Secretariat administers the UN's many programs and policies, ranging from peacekeeping operations to mediating international disputes. It has a staff of approximately 10,000 drawn from about 170 countries. It is headed by the UN's principal officer, the Secretary General. Appointed to a five-year term by the General Assembly, upon the recommendation of the Security Council, the Secretary General's chief responsibilities include bringing before the Security Council matters of peace and security. The position of Secretary General has been held by seven very different statesmen, most of whom left their distinctive stamp on the office and the broader United Nations. The tenure of the first Secretary General, Trygve Lie of Norway (1946–53), was a controversial one, coinciding with the beginnings of the Cold War and growing tensions on the Security Council. He irritated the Truman administration with his suggestion that the People's Republic of China be seated in the United Nations, and his handling of the Korean crisis incensed the Soviet Union, which saw Lie as favoring US aims in the Cold War. But he established a number of important precedents that strengthened his office, such as establishing the authority of the Secretary General to bring matters before the Security Council at any time. His tenure also ended in controversy. The Soviet Union sought to block his effort to secure a second term in 1951 and the United States insisted on his reappointment. As a compromise he was given General Assembly authorization to continue for another three years, but he resigned in late 1952.

Lie was replaced by Dag Hammarskjöld of Sweden (1953–61), who, in the estimation of many observers, stands as the most dynamic Secretary General in its history. As Brian Urquhart has shown in his comprehensive biography *Hammarskjöld*, the second Secretary General left his personal stamp on the UN. He was an activist leader of the UN Secretariat, traveling widely and personally plunging into crises, pursuing what he liked to call "preventive diplomacy." One of his most important legacies came in the area of peacekeeping. In the Suez crisis of 1956 he aided in halting the use of force by Israel, France, and Great Britain against Egypt and, under the UN's mandate, dispatched a United Nations Emergency Force (UNEF) to the region—the first ever mobilized by the UN. In 1958 he established the UN Observation Group in Lebanon, containing the crisis there and facilitating the withdrawal of the American and British troops. He also sought to address the problems stemming from decolonization. In December 1959 and January 1960 he visited 21 countries and territories in Africa. The newly liberated Congo, suffering the consequences of harsh Belgian rule and entangled in the politics of the Cold War, asked the UN for help. It faced the re-intervention of Belgian troops, an army mutiny, and the secession of its southernmost province of Katanga. The UN responded by sending a large peacekeeping force, with Hammarskjöld in overall charge of operations. The mission became enmeshed in the controversies of the Cold War and the Soviet Union demanded the replacement of Hammarskjöld with a *troika*, a group of three administrators. While on a mission to Katanga seeking a cease-fire he and 15 others perished when their plane crashed in September 1961.

Hammarskjöld's successor, U Thant of Burma (1961–1972), was the first Secretary General from Asia, his appointment also revealing the increasing power and influence of the developing world. His low-key

leadership and administrative style stood in contrast to that of his predecessor. Nonetheless, he was active in the search for a settlement of a
number of high-profile disputes, seeking to mediate the Cuban Missile
Crisis of 1962, dispatching peacekeepers to the Cyprus crisis of 1964,
and negotiating the cease-fire in the India-Pakistan War of 1965. His
tenure was also marked by controversy. The decision to withdraw UN
peacekeepers from the Sinai in 1967 at the request of Egypt was blamed
by some for precipitating the Arab-Israeli war of 1967. One of Thant's
chief concerns remained the American war in Southeast Asia, where he
sought a negotiated solution, provoking Washington's displeasure. His
tenure also coincided with increased UN concern for economic and social questions effecting members from the developing world. These
states became a majority in the General Assembly during his terms.

The fourth Secretary General, Kurt Waldheim of Austria (1972–81),
took office in a time of increasing tumult. His early years focused on
the 1971 India-Pakistan dispute over Bangladesh, reestablishing peacekeeping forces in the Middle East, a renewed effort to resolve the Cyprus dispute, and the continued search for peace in Vietnam. He also
played a role in seeking an end to the Iranian hostage crisis (1979–
1981), and supported efforts to mediate the Iran-Iraq war (1980–1988),
and the Soviet-Afghan war (1979–1989). Waldheim, although coming
from the developed world, sought to make concessions to the Third
World and lent support to many of its aspirations. This did not protect
him, however, from criticism from the developing world, even as his tenure coincided with the proclamation of the Third World's New International Economic Order in 1974, which he was accused of impeding.
His efforts to secure an unprecedented third term were blocked by a
Chinese Security Council veto in 1981. He was thereafter elected president of Austria in 1986, despite the revelation that he had been a German army officer in a unit that committed atrocities in Yugoslavia and
Greece during World War II.

Waldheim's replacement, Javier Perez de Cuellar of Peru (1982–91)
was Secretary General during a period of great optimism for the United
Nations. He oversaw the waning of the Cold War and the formation of
the UN coalition in the 1990–1991 Gulf crisis. His tenure also coincided with the growth of UN responsibilities such as the expansion of
peacekeeping operations into Central America and Africa. He brokered
the cease-fire that concluded the Iran-Iraq War and oversaw the with-

drawal of Soviet forces from Afghanistan. He expedited the Cambodian peace accords in 1991 and was active in working toward the El Salvadoran peace pact in 1992.

The sixth Secretary General, Boutros Boutros-Ghali of Egypt (1992–97), was the first Secretary General from Africa and the Arab world. He assumed his post during a time of transition. His tenure included some of the UN's most controversial and tumultuous years as UN peacekeeping operations multiplied around the world. During his term, the UN suffered severe setbacks in the Balkans, where the UN's peacekeepers and safe havens were frequently overpowered; in Somalia, where UN efforts at nation building were overwhelmed; and Rwanda, where the UN was criticized for its paralysis in the face of genocide. When the Republicans swept the 1994 midterm elections he came under scrutiny from Senate Foreign Relations Chairman Jesse Helms (R-North Carolina). He then became a focus of partisan dispute during the 1996 US presidential campaign, at one point criticized by both Democrats and Republicans. Boutros-Ghali's memoir *Unvanquished: A U.S.-UN Saga* recounted his story of how the United States blocked his reelection as Secretary General.

Boutros-Ghali's successor, Kofi Annan of Ghana (1997–), is the first black Secretary General, and the first from sub-Saharan Africa. Annan faced challenges from the outset, such as establishing United Nations involvement in post-conflict Kosovo, overseeing East Timor's path to independence, and aiding emergency efforts to broker a peace accord between Israel and the Palestinians. But perhaps the most perilous challenge Annan faced was the Iraq crisis of 2002–03 and its aftermath. Over the opposition of key members of the Security Council, the United States and Britain went to war in Iraq in March 2003, resulting in an Anglo-American occupation of Iraq, with little UN input.

The International Court of Justice. Often referred to as the World Court, the International Court of Justice is the successor to the League's Permanent Court of International Justice. It is the principal judicial organ of the United Nations, meeting in the Peace Palace in the Hague. It is composed of 15 justices, who serve as independent magistrates. They are elected to nine-year terms by the General Assembly and the Security Council. The Court may not include more than one judge of a single nationality. Nine constitute a quorum and questions are decided by a majority of the judges present. It functions as the UN's judicial arm, but it is an independent body, charged with settling legal disputes submitted to it by member nations and delivering advisory opinions on legal questions referred to it by international organs and agencies.

International Economic Institutions. The World Bank and the International Monetary Fund are products of Bretton Woods, created in the context of the breakdown of the global economy during the interwar years. (*See Document No. 8.*) The World Bank is actually the World Bank Group, and includes five financial institutions. (*See Document No. 7.*) The Bank does not make grants, but offers loans. Its stated mission is to provide development assistance, reduce global poverty, facilitate economic growth, and aid in the improvement of global living standards. The capital for the loans is raised by issuing bonds. The International Monetary Fund is a UN specialized agency. It seeks to maintain international monetary stability and often collaborates with the World Bank. Out of these initial institutions was also born the General Agreement on Tariffs and Trade (GATT) in 1947, which sought to promote and regulate world trade. GATT was replaced in 1995 by the World Trade Organization (WTO), a global body formed in 1994 to help harmonize trade rules and practices in an interconnected world. More recently, many have charged that the World Bank and IMF are more interested in protecting capital in the Western developed core than in working toward development on the periphery. As Paul Taylor has shown in *International Organization in the Age of Globalization*, both the World Bank and the IMF, along with the World Trade Organization, have been subjects of a stinging critique by scholars, politicians, and a well-organized global protest movement.

CHAPTER 2

THE UNITED NATIONS AND THE COLD WAR: 1945–1990

The Cold War Determines the Course of the United Nations. The United Nations began with much optimism—much as the League did in the wake of the Versailles Treaty—that the world might now embark upon a new era in relations among states. In the United States, fear of a repetition of Woodrow Wilson's mishandling of the peace led the Roosevelt and Truman administrations to oversell the UN's potential, particularly in the area of collective security. After years of war, the world could be forgiven for succumbing to such optimism, but these unrealistically high expectations were destined to be dashed. The Cold War, which evolved simultaneously with the United Nations, would cool much of the initial optimism and have a profound influence on the first four decades of the UN. East-West tensions would not only play out within the institutions of the UN, but would also at times marginalize the UN and its role in world affairs. As Robert Gregg has explained in *About Face: The United States and the United Nations*, it "was impossible to keep the Cold War out of the UN, and the superpowers, rather than trying to insulate the global forum from the struggle in which they were engaged, turned the UN into a major arena for that struggle."

Nonetheless, the role of the United Nations in keeping the Cold War from becoming a hot war has often been overlooked, and this chapter will demonstrate how the UN at times provided a forum for negotiation and the airing of grievances in a number of Cold War controversies such as Korea, the Cuban Missile Crisis, the Vietnam War, and the Soviet invasion of Afghanistan. In those decades before the United Nations, the world had endured two world wars that claimed more than 75 million lives. In the six decades after the founding of the UN, and with considerable tension among the great powers, another cataclysmic war never occurred, to the surprise and relief of many. Thus one major contribution of the UN may be what has *not* happened in the years since its founding, as opposed to what has. Such achievements are difficult to measure. Initially, it seemed the United Nations might have a decisive influence on the Cold War conflict; it played a role in adjudicating early

Cold War tensions in Iran in 1946, facilitating a Soviet withdrawal. Its participation in the subsequent Korean crisis of 1950, when large numbers of forces were dispatched, nominally under the UN banner, led many to assume that the UN would have some impact on the Cold War. But, in the years after the Korean War, and during some of the most important events of the Cold War, it became apparent that the UN was often a bystander to the crises of the East-West struggle. While successive Secretaries General sought an expanded role for the UN, it often became a mere soap box, issuing non-binding General Assembly declarations about an assortment of Cold War concerns.

Cold War politics frequently disabled the United Nations. One of the early controversies involved admitting new members. Prior to 1955, the United States blocked the admission of states it perceived as little more than Soviet clients such as Albania, Bulgaria, Hungary, and Romania, while the Soviet Union barred pro-Western states such as Austria, Ireland, Japan, and Italy. In key Cold War flashpoints in the years after the Korean War such as Hungary in 1956, the Berlin crisis of 1961, the Cuban Missile Crisis of 1962, the Vietnam War, the Soviet crushing of the Prague Spring movement in 1968, and the Soviet invasion of Afghanistan in 1979, the UN often found itself on the periphery of events. It was not until near the end of the Cold War that it began to play a more effective role in resolving Cold War-related questions, such as its efforts to deescalate the Soviet-Afghan war and reduce Cold War tensions in Central America.

The Cold War made collective action increasingly difficult, as both the United States and the Soviet Union had permanent seats on the Security Council with veto power. In retrospect, the collective response to the Korean crisis was an anomaly, because the Soviet Union had been boycotting the Security Council, thus allowing the US to use the UN to pursue its aims in Korea. The Cold War also had implications for the functioning of the United Nations itself. In some US political circles, the UN increasingly looked like a hotbed of subversion. Adding to the UN's woes was mounting dismay in the United States as it became increasingly clear that, as the composition of the UN changed, Washington could not continue to enlist the UN to support its Cold War aims. The United States held distinct advantages at the UN for the first two decades of the Cold War struggle, as membership and voting patterns favored the US point of view. Thereafter, in part owing to growing UN membership as a result of decolonization, the Soviet Union began to have the advantage in the General Assembly. The United States, which prided itself on having never used the veto in the Security Council during the first quarter century, issued vetoes with increasing frequency thereafter. The Soviet Union, which resorted to the veto numerous times during the first two decades when it felt outnumbered at the UN, issued them less often thereafter, partly because of its success in courting the new members, most of whom came from the decolonizing, or developing, world.

In part because of their dogged pursuit of their Cold War aims, both the US and the USSR squandered numerous opportunities to build the kind of relationships at the United Nations necessary to muster support for their international objectives. From the emergence of the nonaligned movement in the mid-1950s the United States remained uncertain about how to approach the developing world. The war in Vietnam, complicated by Washington's difficulty distinguishing between real and imagined Cold War threats, its willingness to undermine or even overthrow states it perceived as obstacles to its Cold War objectives, and its heavy-hand with states in its chief sphere of interest in Central America and the Caribbean, did much to turn many members of the General Assembly against the United States and its aims. Global economic, trade, and development questions also influenced Cold War perspectives. Many General Assembly members became disillusioned with the US-dominated international economic order (a subject of Chapter 3) and saw the United States as the leading power upholding that order to the detriment of much of the developing world.

The Soviet Union mounted a campaign to court the Third World bloc but often found its efforts undermined by its own behavior abroad and the poor performance of its economy at home. This perception was reinforced by its iron grip on its own internal republics and the satellite states bordering the USSR, by the crushing of the Hungarian uprising in 1956 and the Prague Spring in 1968, the border war with the People's Republic of China in 1969, the invasion of Afghanistan in 1979, and its bullying behavior toward both allies and adversaries. These events sent shock waves through the international system, demonstrating to many that friendship with the Soviet Union often required slavish ideological conformity. The so-called Brezhnev Doctrine, the West's name for Soviet premier Leonid Brezhnev's declaration that countries in the Soviet orbit had only "limited sovereignty" and that the Kremlin alone had the right to decide the nature of their political regimes, revealed to many that the USSR reserved the right to intervene anywhere its brand of socialism was threatened. To many this revealed that Moscow, too, would deploy its considerable power to pursue its narrow aims and objectives in the Cold War struggle.

Both the United States and the USSR increasingly became enforcers of the geopolitical status quo (as each perceived it). They sought to perpetuate it in their favor at almost any cost, reflexively quashing any real or perceived threats to that order. Many of the newly independent nations of the Third World remained wary of this superpower competition. In part, it was this disenchantment with the superpowers' inability to see the world as it was, not narrowly filtered through a Cold War lens, that motivated so many emerging nations to avoid the conflict and instead join the nonaligned movement.

The newly emerging nations resisted the control of either power bloc. This refusal to take sides vexed officials in both Moscow and Washington. "When the UN instead gave support to the idea of moral equivalence when it was not actually endorsing Soviet-supported causes and clients," Robert Gregg has noted, "the United States tended to react as if the global body were legitimizing evil rather than simply reflecting the interests of its members." Many US officials, such as Secretary of State John Foster Dulles (1953–59), saw neutralism as immoral and reacted with alarm when nonaligned nations praised the USSR. Many nonaligned nations did tilt toward the USSR or the People's Republic of China, but the West rarely acknowledged that this often was a reaction to having been colonized by a Western power. Emerging nations also realized the potential of obtaining aid from either or both of the competing superpowers by adroitly playing one off against the other. As the UN scholar Evan Luard has observed, the nonaligned nations had enough sophistication to be dubious of the blandishments offered by both sides in the Cold War.

The United Nations and the Korean Crisis. Korea provided the stage for one of the most important events in the history of the United Nations. That an event with such international implications should happen in Korea, a place previously known as the Hermit Kingdom and seen as a backwater in world politics, demonstrated the increasingly global nature of the Cold War struggle, as well as the far-flung responsibilities of the new world organization. The war, which began when North Korean forces crossed the 38th parallel on June 25,

1950, marked the first time that the United Nations invoked chapter VII (*see Document No. 10*) of the UN Charter to authorize force. It also led to the introduction—at the instigation of US Secretary of State Dean Acheson—of the Uniting for Peace Resolution in November 1950 (*see Document No. 11*), where the General Assembly sought to circumvent Soviet vetoes in the Security Council. The Korean War significantly aggravated the tensions of the Cold War and poisoned the debate over the admission of mainland China, delaying its membership for two decades. And, as the stalemate on the Korean peninsula continued, it ratcheted up tensions between the UN and the US and revealed that, in the context of the Cold War, they would not always see eye to eye.

During the twentieth century, Korea, owing to its strategic location astride the sea lanes between Japan and mainland Asia, was coveted by Russia, Japan, and China, and ultimately the United States. As Bruce Cumings has argued in *The Origins of the Korean War*, near the end of the Second World War Korea, which for the previous four decades had been a Japanese colony, was arbitrarily divided at the 38th parallel. Initial negotiations contemplated the ultimate reunification of the peninsula, but the US and USSR subsequently established antagonistic governments in the North and South, precluding the possibility of an easy—or early—resolution. Washington created a separate South Korean government under Syngman Rhee, while in North Korea, a separate regime emerged, headed by Kim Il-sung and supported by the Soviet Union. In 1947 the United Nations General Assembly created the UN Temporary Commission on Korea (UNTCOK) to supervise elections for the entire peninsula, but when access to the North was denied, elections were held only in the South, with the claim to represent all of Korea. The elections, of dubious credibility, returned a strong majority for US-backed Syngman Rhee. In 1948 the United Nations created a new UN Commission on Korea (UNCOK), empowering it with responsibility for unification and overseeing the withdrawal of foreign forces.

Before this could be completed, North Korea attacked in June 1950 and overran much of South Korea. The UN Security Council met in emergency session, which the Soviet Union had been boycotting to protest the UN's refusal to seat the People's Republic of China. President Truman seized the opportunity to use the United Nations to legitimize the Western response to North Korea's aggression. With the US leading the way, a series of resolutions passed the Security Council before the Soviet ambassador, Jacob Malik, could return from his boycott. Scholars such as John Moore and Jerry Pubantz, authors of *To Create a New World: American Presidents and the United Nations,* see Truman's use of the United Nations as an achievement for the international community, as more than 15 nations ultimately came to supply forces of some description, helping the United States demonstrate support for collective security. However, as William Stueck has shown in *The Korean War: an International History,* 90 percent of the forces engaged were either U.S. or South Korean, and George Mazuzan, the author of *Warren Austin at the UN, 1946–1953* has argued that Truman used the UN to marshal support for narrow Cold War objectives.

After the UN forces engineered a daring landing at Inchon and pushed North Korean forces back across the 38th parallel, Truman and the UN commander, General Douglas MacArthur, used the 1948 General Assembly resolution as a rationale to unify the entire peninsula. Accordingly, UN forces marched deep into North Korea, approaching the border with China. The newly established (1949) People's Republic of China (PRC) grew alarmed over the presence of United Nations forces so near its border and resolved not to allow the establishment of a unified Korean republic created by the US. Stanley Meisler, in *The United Nations: the First Fifty Years,* has explained that MacArthur (who ignored various warnings from Chinese Foreign Minister Chou En-lai) planned to follow the same route into Manchuria that the Japanese did in 1931 and reawakened Chinese fears of foreign domination. In November, forces from the People's Republic of China intervened in Korea, at one point driving United Nations forces below the 38th parallel. Ultimately, after months of fighting, a bloody stalemate ensued with heavy casualties on all sides.

The Korean War brought to the surface serious difficulties between Washington and the United Nations. In response to the Chinese intervention, faced with the prospect of a wider war and confronted with Truman's intemperate talk of using nuclear weapons, a majority of UN members, following the lead of Canadian Foreign Minister Lester Pearson, sought a cease-fire and UN-sponsored negotiations that would include mainland China. William Stueck has argued that, as the months passed, the UN was less and less a crude instrument of US aims in Korea and increasingly a restraining influence over some of the more extreme impulses of MacArthur and Truman. United Nations efforts to resolve the conflict met with hostile opposition from the US, which sought to punish China for its intervention in Korea and for the heavy casualties suffered by UN forces. As the stalemate in Korea dragged on, US support for the United Nations declined. At the beginning of 1951 the General Assembly created a cease-fire commission to search for a settlement, but efforts at a negotiated solution drove a deeper rift between Truman and MacArthur, precipitating the president's dismissal of the flamboyant General in April 1951. By the summer of 1953, the combatants agreed to an armistice, leaving the question of the unification of the Korean Peninsula in the hands of the UN.

The Korean War became the most important test the United Nations faced since its birth in 1945. In inspiring the Uniting for Peace Resolution of November 1950, it tested the flexibility of the UN Charter. But more important, the Korean War had devastating human consequences. Four million Koreans died, three million of them civilians. Korea remains an area of potential crisis and UN concern. Nearly 40,000 US troops remain in Korea, technically as United Nations forces. The war also left behind one of the most unfortunate legacies of the Cold War, as Korea remains divided at the 38th parallel, with an isolated state in the North possessing a nuclear capability.

The United Nations and Cold War Flashpoints: Hungary, Cuba, Vietnam. The division of Korea, and the 1953 UN-sponsored armistice, concluded the hot war between the Communist North and the capitalist South, but the Cold War between the Soviet Union and the United States continued. Although the United Nations played an active role in the Korean conflict, it was frequently marginalized in other areas of Cold War tension where the superpowers made clear that they would not allow international involvement. One such area was Eastern Europe, where in the early years of the Cold War the Soviet Union established that it would not allow any UN involvement in a region considered essential to its security. In February of 1956, only three years after Stalin's death, Soviet premier Nikita Khrushchev denounced his predecessor in frank terms in a speech before a congress of the Communist Party of the USSR. Partly in response to Khrushchev's explosive remarks, the Hungarian communist regime allowed into its inner circle Imre Nagy, a moderate reformer, who subsequently denounced the Warsaw Pact and declared Hungarian neutrality in the Cold War.

Moscow responded with a brazen military intervention. Nagy appealed to the United Nations for help, but the simultaneous invasion of Egypt over Suez undermined the efforts of the West to keep the focus on Hungary. The UN also found that it could do little about Hungary because of the Soviet veto on the Security Council. Instead, the General Assembly, in emergency session and employing the Uniting for Peace strategy, passed a revised version of a Security Council resolution, affirming Hungary's right to self-determination and calling for the withdrawal of Soviet forces. Yet, as Stanley Meisler has argued, the Hungarian crisis revealed the UN's increasing impotence in the face of superpower opposition. Moscow prosecuted Nagy in secret and summarily executed him, installing Janos Kadar, thereafter known as the "Butcher of Budapest," as the new leader of the Hungarian Communist Party. Moreover, Hungary established an unfortunate precedent for the United Nations, as it would play an even more muted role during the subsequent Soviet crushing of the Prague Spring rising in neighboring Czechoslovakia in 1968.

In the aftermath of the Hungarian crisis, Cold War tensions continued to escalate. The controversy over the USSR's launch of the earth-orbiting satellite, Sputnik, in October 1957 and the shooting down of an American U-2 surveillance plane in May 1960 over Russia added to the climate of unease. The 1960 crisis in the Congo further aggravated Cold War tensions and resulted in the USSR withholding a portion of its UN dues, precipitating a fiscal crisis at the UN. It expressed its anger over Hammarskjöld's handling of the Congo crisis (Moscow accused the Secretary General of taking the West's side in the Congo) by demanding the Secretary General's resignation and replacement by a three-member administrative *troika*. In April 1961, the United States helped launch the Bay of Pigs invasion against Cuba, seeking to topple the revolutionary regime of Fidel Castro using anti-Castro exiles. The invasion failed, but it set in motion a series of events that laid the groundwork for one of the most dramatic confrontations of the Cold War.

In response to the Bay of Pigs debacle, the USSR sought some means of deterring another US invasion of Cuba. After the failure of the Bay of Pigs, the US launched Operation Mongoose, a covert operation to destabilize Cuba and overthrow or kill Castro. Khrushchev sought not only to reinforce Castro, but to dramatically challenge the US strategic advantage in the region. In October 1962 US intelligence discovered Soviet intermediate range nuclear missiles in Cuba. The US Ambassador to the UN, Adlai Stevenson, presented Washington's case before the Security Council and both Stevenson and Premier Khrushchev looked to Secretary General U Thant to play a possible intermediary role. Even

President John F. Kennedy was willing to have the UN play a role in the crisis so long as the UN could take responsibility, and deflect public criticism of him, in the event of the US making unpopular concessions. The UN played an important role as the US sought to influence world opinion and keep communications open between the superpowers. But the actual resolution of the crisis came during secret negotiations between US and Soviet officials outside the UN. As former colonies became member nations, the UN's composition—and aims—changed radically. The Cuban Missile Crisis would represent one of the last times, for some time to come, that the United States would use the world body to seek the support of the international community on an important matter.

The role of the United Nations, and its relationship with the United States, would be substantially affected by the Vietnam War. To avoid a repetition of its problems with the UN during the Korean War, successive US administrations sought to exclude the UN from its war in Indochina. The UN would thus have almost no impact on the war in Southeast Asia, and its influence would remain negligible throughout the conflict. The General Assembly passed a series of non-binding resolutions seeking to end the war and was often critical of US policy, but the Security Council remained paralyzed throughout, as both the US and USSR threatened to veto any initiatives they deemed contrary to their interests in Southeast Asia. The United Nations was further stymied because neither North nor South Vietnam held membership in the UN.

Throughout the crisis in Southeast Asia, Secretary General U Thant remained optimistic that a negotiated settlement might be reached. He sought just such a settlement several times. Thant also proposed an international conference on Southeast Asia to be held in Geneva, similar to the one held there on Indochina in 1954, which helped facilitate the French exit from the region. In Washington, President Lyndon Johnson and administration officials grew increasingly dismayed over what they perceived as Thant's meddling in a war that was, to them, clearly a matter of vital US interest. Johnson and many of his senior advisors resented that Thant, and many member states as well, did not wholeheartedly support US aims in Indochina. From the perspective of Thant—a Burmese national with a strong commitment to avoiding an escalation in Southeast Asia or the possibility of a wider war among the great powers (as was the case in Korea), any effort in the search for peace was worthwhile. Furthermore, the composition of the General Assembly, as noted above, had undergone a tremendous transformation since the Korean War, with the majority of members now from decolonizing and/or developing nations. This change in the General Assembly occurred simultaneously with the growing perception at the UN that the American war in Indochina was nothing more than a continuation of the imperial struggle in Southeast Asia, now in the guise of the Cold War.

In the summer of 1965 Thant approached Britain and France with his "Rangoon Initiative." It sought to have the other Western members of the Security Council take the lead in a UN effort to explore possibilities for ending the war. Ambassador Stevenson was always more receptive than other members of the US administration to a UN role in resolving the war. While in London to explore Thant's plan, Stevenson died suddenly at the age of 65, and whatever remote hope the Rangoon Initiative had died with him. Stevenson, a two-time Democratic Party nominee for the presidency, was the most prominent US ambassador Washington ever sent to the UN, and his death was a blow to the stature of the US mission to the UN. To maintain a semblance of this prestige President Johnson persuaded Supreme Court Justice Arthur Goldberg to step down from the bench and take up Stevenson's duties at the UN, but enthusiasm for a UN initiative on Vietnam had been lost.

While Thant remained committed to a negotiated solution, his efforts continually ran afoul of officials in Washington committed to pursuing their own objectives in Vietnam and neighboring states. Both Presidents Johnson and Richard M. Nixon grew increasingly exasperated by even the hint of a UN exploratory effort to negotiate an end to the conflict. Thant stepped down as Secretary General in 1972 and died in 1974. The Vietnam War, like the Hungarian crisis of 1956, again revealed the UN's limitations in dealing with any international crisis involving permanent members of the Security Council.

The United Nations and the Two Chinas Controversy. China is a proud nation with 5,000 years of recorded history. It encompasses one of the largest land masses in the world and is home to the largest population on earth. But for at least a century, beginning with the Opium Wars (1839–1842) against the faltering Ch'ing Dynasty, China was subjected to increasing exploitation by outside powers. The horrors of the Opium Wars were followed by the bloody Taiping Rebellion (1850–1864), upheavals spawned by intervention and increasing economic penetration by Western imperial powers throughout the late nineteenth century, the Boxer Rebellion (1898–1900), Japanese imperialism, and the Chinese Civil War.

As Robert Hilderbrand has shown in *Dumbarton Oaks: The Origins of the United Nations and the Search for Postwar Security*, during the Second World War President Roosevelt believed that China would emerge from that conflict as a great power. The US fought hard against both British and Soviet opposition to China's inclusion as a member of the Four Policemen and, ultimately, a permanent seat on the Security Council. Roosevelt sought to aid the reemergence of China as a great power with regional and global responsibilities. Mainland China, still led by Generalissimo Chiang Kai-shek, held the permanent seat on the Security Council during the first four years of the United Nations. He held it for the next 22 years, even after Mao Zedong declared the People's Republic of China on the mainland and Chiang and his Nationalist state had fled across the straits of Taiwan to Formosa (now Taiwan).

The United Nations, with strong US backing, continued to uphold the seating of the Taiwan-based Nationalist regime on the Security Council, despite Soviet efforts to replace it with the mainland. As mentioned earlier, the Soviets went so far as to boycott the Security Council over the issue in 1950, unwittingly allowing the US-led UN intervention in Korea. After the Korean War, and throughout the 1950s and 1960s, mainland China became an emotional issue at the UN and in American politics. But, with the changing composition of the General Assembly, and gyrations in the global geopolitical situation such as the Sino-Soviet split, representatives from the People's Republic took their seats in the United Nations (including the permanent seat on the Security Council) in 1971, 22 years after achieving victory on the mainland. This represented a long overdue concession to reality, as at the time of admission its population exceeded 800 million, while Taiwan's was only 15 million.

The admission of mainland China into the United Nations meant that both the US and the USSR (the Sino-Soviet split was now complete) would increasingly have to compete with a rising Asiatic superpower with aspirations to lead the developing world, unencumbered by imperial baggage or a history of colonial economic exploitation. The People's Republic has been gradually evolving as one of the world's superpowers, becoming increasingly influential in regional and world affairs. Once in the UN, mainland China worked to promote the interests of the Third World, but in time its support for developing nations became more rhetorical than substantive. China relished its position as the only Asian superpower and followed patterns of behavior previously charted by other great powers—such as the US and the USSR—over matters it considers of primary interest, such as Tibet and Taiwan, which China insists are internal matters, beyond the jurisdiction of UN interference. At the same time, China's desire to participate in global economic institutions such as the International Monetary Fund, the World Bank, and the World Trade Organization, demonstrates the growing trend of China seeking to become a full participant in world affairs and to use global institutions to serve its objectives.

Cold War Tensions Strain the US-UN Relationship. The US's Cold War approach to the United Nations developed over time. To varying degrees the Truman, Eisenhower, and Kennedy administrations often sought to reconcile the goals of America's Cold War containment strategy with its approach to the UN. These administrations all believed that the need to wage the Cold War on their own terms far outweighed the broader interests of the UN or the international community. As UN membership continued to grow, upheaval in the developing world increasingly became a part of the Cold War. Many national movements had been radicalized by years of colonial rule, repression, economic exploitation, the denial of sovereignty, and the often violent struggles for independence against the colonial powers. Many peoples not only desired political freedom, but also economic and cultural independence, often through radical or revolutionary means. To many in the newly-independent world, the Western powers, with their imperial pasts, represented an obstacle to reordering world politics. Thus, the political coloration of the post-imperial era tended to have a distinctly anti-Western hue.

The initial pro-Western, European-influenced composition of the early United Nations increasingly gave way to a membership driven by the interests of its African, Asian, Middle Eastern, and Latin American members. The growing perception in much of the General Assembly was that the United States and its Western allies were a barrier to further efforts at national liberation and self-determination. As Robert Gregg has argued, for many UN members "imperialism was imperialism, regardless of the rationale offered in its defense, and it was often US intervention to halt the spread of communism that produced the greatest resentment." On the other hand, from the perspective of the West, Third World national liberation struggles often appeared to be

Soviet-inspired. Moscow enjoyed relatively better relations with the UN's caucus of Third World nations known as the Group of 77, although Evan Luard suggests this was perhaps more the result of Soviet skill in courting the developing nations by supporting decolonization than support for Moscow's objectives.

Latin America, with many nations struggling with chronic social problems that were often the legacies of the colonial social structure, was seen in the US as a potentially destabilizing theater of the Cold War. As demonstrated in Cuba, the United States faced some of its most vexing Cold War problems within its own primary area of interest—the Western Hemisphere—where Washington's Cold War application of the Monroe Doctrine rationalized the right to intervene in the affairs of other nations in the region. While most Latin American states were developing nations and often joined with other regions in supporting Third World development schemes, they largely supported many of Washington's political aims in the Cold War struggle. This helps to explain US reactions to the apostasy of Cuba and, for a brief time, Chile, and later Nicaragua.

The nations of Central America and the Caribbean, because of their proximity to the United States and the US strategic interest in the Panama Canal, aroused particular concern in Washington. In Guatemala in 1954, in the midst of a United Nations effort to resolve tensions between the Eisenhower administration and the elected government of Jacobo Arbenz, the United States, working with the Organization of American States (OAS), overthrew the Guatemalan government, replacing it with a military regime supportive of US aims. In so doing, it also began a long and bloody insurgency in the country, which would persist for the next four decades and take the lives of more than 100,000 Guatemalans. In neighboring El Salvador, the US backed a series of repressive military juntas while underdevelopment and human rights abuses fueled a rising tide of discontent, and an armed insurgency challenged Washington's clients there. In Chile, Washington paid no heed to UN complaints following the US-supported overthrow of the elected president Salvador Allende Gossens and the widespread violations of humans rights that followed.

In Nicaragua, however, the revolutionary Sandinista movement succeeded in 1979 in overthrowing the local strongman, Anastasio Somoza, a longtime US client. What followed in Nicaragua revealed the complexity of the US approach to matters in its area of primary interest. It also revealed the futility of UN efforts to resolve tensions when US and UN objectives diverged. Events in Nicaragua after 1979 followed a pattern similar to events in Castro's Cuba after 1958, but differing in a number of important details. Like Cuba, the revolutionary regime in Nicaragua, by achieving power, utilized its membership in the United Nations to promote its cause and interests, and also as a forum to criticize US threats against it. Whereas mere rebel movements in the region, such as the insurgencies in Guatemala and El Salvador, were powerless to use the UN in such a manner, recognized governments, with *de facto* and *de jure* legitimacy, faced no such obstacles.

In the context of the Cold War, such distinctions appeared to matter little to Washington, which financed an insurgency in Nicaragua—the Contra rebels—aimed to pressure, and perhaps overthrow, the Sandinista regime. The US also went so far as mining Nicaraguan harbors and launching other covert operations to destabilize the Nicaraguan economy. But Nicaragua, a sovereign state recognized by the United Nations, lodged a series of complaints at the UN against US actions and also before the International Court of Justice (ICJ), charging the United States with violations of its sovereignty. In 1986 the ICJ ruled in Nicaragua's favor (*see Document No. 12*), while at the Security Council the US vetoed seven resolutions critical of its actions in the region. Nevertheless, the United Nations remained powerless to do much about the crisis in Central America so long as the Cold War continued and so long as the United States wielded the veto.

Controversies at the UN over US policy in the region did, however, deepen the rift between the Reagan administration (1981–89) and the United Nations, as Washington disregarded World Court rulings and also pulled out of the United Nations Educational, Scientific, and Cultural Organization (UNESCO). Yet, as Cold War tensions receded in 1989 and 1990, the United States began to offer support for regional and international efforts at conflict resolution in Central America, with the UN subsequently playing an important role (a subject of Chapter 6) by dispatching observer groups, election monitors, and aiding in the demobilization of opposing military factions.

The United Nations and the Soviet-Afghan War. In April 1978 a coup in the remote landlocked central Asian nation of Afghanistan provoked a chain of events that, over the course of a quarter century of conflict, would lead to the intervention there of the Soviet Union and, two decades later, of the United States. Moscow sought to prop up a friendly regime on its southern border recently brought to power as a result of the 1978 coup. Fearing that a tide of Islamic militancy would sweep through those Soviet republics with large Muslim populations, Moscow intervened in Afghanistan with 75,000 troops in December 1979. Soviet good faith toward the global south was rightly called into question, and much of the goodwill Moscow had sought to build up with the developing world at the UN was shattered by the invasion of Afghanistan, a sovereign state and one of the earliest Asian members of the UN.

The United Nations became involved early, with the Security Council meeting on January 5, 1980 to address the invasion, but there was little it could do to halt the fighting in the face of the Soviet threat to veto any action against its intervention. In February 1981 UN Secretary General Kurt Waldheim dispatched Javier Perez de Cuellar, a future Secretary General, to mediate an end to the Soviet-Afghan conflict, but the Security Council remained powerless to stop the fighting or to pressure the Soviets to withdraw. Instead, the UN worked to prevent the conflict from escalating into a wider war, potentially involving the superpowers. It also moved to alleviate the humanitarian consequences of the war, particularly the massive refugee crisis that was threatening to destabilize neighboring Pakistan. The US became increasingly engaged in the conflict, sending aid of various sorts to almost any group claiming to represent anti-Soviet forces based in both Afghanistan and Pakistan.

The Afghan conflict again revealed the obstacles the United Nations faced in crises involving permanent members of the Security Council. It was only with the eventual cooperation of Moscow, after Gorbachev's coming to power in March 1985, that the UN made some progress toward a resolution. He began searching for an exit strategy, seeking to use the UN as a vehicle for withdrawal. This paralleled Gorbachev's policy of so-called "new thinking" in foreign affairs, where the USSR would pursue better relations with the West and a more constructive role within the UN as part of his policy of *glasnost* (increasing openness in Soviet life) and *perestroika* (the reform and restructuring of the Soviet system). In an article in Pravda in 1987 Gorbachev articulated his desire to have the United Nations play a larger role in Soviet foreign policy. He therefore fully backed the UN-initiated Geneva negotiations seeking an end to the bloody stalemate in Afghanistan. The process bore fruit in 1989 when the Geneva Accords between Afghanistan and Pakistan were announced—with the US and the USSR as guarantors—facilitating a withdrawal of Soviet forces.

Although the UN had played a role in ending the Soviet-Afghan conflict, resolution was more a consequence of Moscow's desire to extract itself from the stalemate and the result of the slow winding down of Cold War tensions. The Geneva process succeeded in slowly extracting Soviet forces from Afghanistan, but it did little to achieve an internal Afghan settlement. The fighting among factions there continued, a struggle largely ignored in the West after the Soviet withdrawal. The Afghan conflict would have profound repercussions, many of them felt far beyond the region. Emphasis on the Cold War masked a multiplicity of other factors at work in the region, few of them anticipated by those involved in the ghastly struggle. Washington's effort to aid extreme Islamic groups to wage war against Soviet forces encouraged the phenomenon of "blowback," a term used by the American CIA to describe the unintended consequences of US policies. In the aftermath of the withdrawal of Soviet forces from Afghanistan, many of the erstwhile allies of the United States would become adversaries, redirecting their wrath toward their former benefactors.

With the removal of Soviet forces the world's attention moved on to other matters and much of the world lost interest in the ultimate outcome of the Afghan conflict. Afghanistan was abandoned to its fate. Various armed factions, many of them fostered by the United States and its chief regional ally, Pakistan, continued the bloody struggle, with massive casualties on all sides. In 1992, the former Soviet client Mohammed Najibullah was overthrown, subsequently captured, and butchered to death by formerly US-backed fundamentalist forces. The various elements within the opposition Mujahideen, divided by cultural, religious, tribal, and linguistic differences, fell out in a bloody and protracted civil conflict. In 1996, the hardline fundamentalist Taliban faction, a descendent of the US-backed Mujahideen, took power in Kabul and continued the armed struggle against various opponents. The largest of these, now calling itself the Northern Alliance, was made up of many disparate elements, some of whom had been on the Soviet side in the 1979–1989 war. The Taliban impeded United Nations humanitarian operations, particularly for women, and the regime gave sanctuary to hardline groups such as the international terror network Al-Qaeda. Some members of this network had received encouragement and support from the United States during the waning years of the Cold War. Responding to the September 11, 2001 attacks on New York and Washington, the United States intervened in Afghanistan on the side of the Northern Alliance, deposed the Taliban regime and, less successfully, tried to destroy Al-Qaeda's organization and forces loyal to it.

The United Nations' role in post-Taliban Afghanistan remains rigidly circumscribed by US forces there, which continue to seek a way to build some semblance of state infrastructure in a region shattered by more than a quarter century of war and superpower intervention. Ironically, only a little more than a decade after the end of the Soviet-Afghan war, the United States found itself at war in Afghanistan, fighting some of its former proxies, many of whom had received US backing against Soviet forces only two decades before. The United States also made common cause with factions it sought to oppose during the years of the Soviet intervention and, perhaps most ironic of all, found itself in a position very similar to that once pursued by Moscow: nation building in Afghanistan and seeking to contain Islamic radicalism. In a further bizarre twist, in the hope of maintaining some semblance of order in the war torn country, the US began subsidizing various warlords of dubious character, many of whom had human rights records little better than the Taliban regime. What long-term role the United Nations will play in Afghanistan remains to be seen. But the US has depended upon the UN from the earliest days of its involvement in Afghanistan to once again provide humanitarian support and relief for refugee populations, as well as for organizing various Afghan political factions into something resembling a legitimate national government.

The United Nations and the End of the Cold War. As Gorbachev's reform efforts continued, he increasingly saw the United Nations playing a pivotal role in the revolution he was planning for Soviet foreign policy. As Archie Brown has explained in *The Gorbachev Factor*, such a move also aided Gorbachev's strategy of shifting the locus of national power away from the Soviet military industrial complex to a new sphere of public and civic culture. Following a 1987 speech to the UN about new thinking in Soviet foreign policy, he addressed the General Assembly in December 1988 (*see Document No. 13*) where he stated that "force or the threat of force can no longer be an instrument of foreign policy," thus signaling a radical departure from the Brezhnev Doctrine. Gorbachev stunned the General Assembly by announcing drastic cuts in the Soviet military presence in Eastern Europe and along the

Chinese border—moves that subsequently allowed Soviet satellites to choose their own paths. His remarks clearly spelled out that a new era was dawning in the international system, one that would enable him to embark upon deep, unilateral, arms reductions and a retreat from dogmatic Cold War ideology in foreign affairs, while refocusing on global challenges such as underdevelopment, environmental degradation, and terrorism. His address stood as the clearest example yet that the end of the Cold War was at hand.

At many junctures throughout the Cold War, the United Nations seemed irrelevant. That Gorbachev should announce before the General Assembly what, in hindsight, appears to have amounted to a unilateral declaration of the end of the Cold War, underscored that the Soviet leader thought the UN should now take center stage as the focal point of a new international system, a system which had been postponed by the advent of the Cold War in 1945. In retrospect, Gorbachev sought to initiate a revolution in world politics, one that would end the stalemated bipolarity of the Cold War era and usher in a new world order with the United Nations at its center.

Gorbachev's so-called "new thinking" about the world included support for expanded UN peacekeeping operations, the revival of the moribund Military Staff Committee, expanded use of the International Court of Justice, and an enhanced role for both the General Assembly and the Security Council. But what might have been a new beginning for the United Nations turned out to be a lost opportunity, as the Soviet Union, on the verge of disintegration, was too enfeebled to take the lead on such reforms, and his challenge was met with suspicion and shortsightedness in the West. The Cold War bipolar balance of power would yield to a new international order, not so much based upon the United Nations, but rather on American primacy.

The end of the Cold War nevertheless resulted in the UN playing a hugely expanded role in world affairs, in many cases seeking to resolve crises provoked by the sudden collapse of the Cold War system. The end of the Cold War brought about new demands for peacekeeping as the demise of the bipolar order witnessed a dizzying increase in the number of nation states and conflicts. The breakup of Yugoslavia, for example, not only created (so far) five new members of the United Nations—Slovenia, Croatia, Bosnia-Herzegovina, Macedonia, and a rump state of Yugoslavia (now the Federal Republic of Serbia and Montenegro)—with a possible sixth or even seventh state waiting in the wings to join the community of nations. It also led to a massive UN intervention to separate warring factions, halt ethnic violence, and provide humanitarian relief. Ultimately, UN peacekeepers became involved in Croatia, Bosnia, Kosovo, and Macedonia. The breakup of the USSR in December 1991 initially posed less of a challenge for United Nations peacekeeping and humanitarian efforts, but nonetheless introduced 15 new, or at least reborn, member states—Estonia, Latvia, Lithuania, Armenia, Azerbaijan, Georgia, Kazakhstan, Kyrgyzstan, Moldavia, Tajikistan, Turkmenistan, and Uzbekistan, and also reintroduced more familiar national entities to the UN in new state forms, such as Russia, Ukraine, and Belarus. And, in a development that would have been unthinkable during the life of the USSR, the UN dispatched peacekeepers to contain and stabilize conflicts in the former Soviet republics of Georgia and Tajikistan.

The end of the Cold War heightened optimism at the United Nations about the prospect of creating a new international order with the UN at its core. The UN's role in the 1990–1991 Gulf crisis led many to believe that, with the Cold War over, the paralysis which had plagued the United Nations, and particularly the Security Council, would now lift. Much of this optimism, initially a product of the euphoria surrounding the end of the Cold War and the UN's cooperation over Kuwait, would soon be tested in Bosnia, Somalia, and Rwanda, and by numerous other challenges and crises the UN would face in the years since the end of the Cold War.

CHAPTER 3

THE UNITED NATIONS TRANSFORMED: THE EMERGENCE OF THE THIRD WORLD

Decolonization and the Era of Dag Hammarskjöld, 1953–1961. One of the most important aspects of the history of the United Nations is the division between the developed core and the developing periphery, also known as the "First" and "Third" worlds, or the global North and South (because so many of the developing countries were situated in the Southern Hemisphere). During its first decade, the United Nations was largely Western-dominated. The Security Council reflected the views of the Western world, with its permanent membership consisting of four largely white states with European cultural ties and one Asian state, Nationalist China, or Taiwan, essentially a Western-created client. The broader world of the infant UN was still very much a colonial one. The General Assembly, with 51 member states in 1945, had grown to only 60 by the beginning of 1955.

Of the original member states, only two, Liberia and Ethiopia, came from sub-Saharan black Africa (as distinct from the white-ruled state of South Africa) and only three states from Asia: China, the Philippines, and India. (India was allowed to join the UN in 1945 although it would not become independent of Britain until 1947). At the end of the UN's first year, 39 of the 51 member states, or 75 percent, came from a Western, European, or Latin American cultural background. Latin American states, while many of them of "developing" status, usually supported US or Western interests and, for political purposes, most belonged to the Western bloc during the early years.

At its tenth anniversary in 1955, membership stood at 60, with only Liberia and Ethiopia still representing sub-Saharan black Africa, and only eight states from Asia. Forty-two of the 60 member states, or 70 percent, came from Western, European, or Latin American backgrounds. Despite the East-West Cold War divide, the United States, its allies, and client states could still depend on healthy majorities in the General Assembly to promote their interests at the UN.

By 1965, the beginning of the UN's third decade, the General Assembly was undergoing a transformation. In the preceding decade the UN's membership had nearly doubled, to 118, with a majority of 63 states from non-Western or non-European backgrounds, including 30 from Africa. The West lost control of the General Assembly and, with it, many of the other institutions of the UN. In 1970, as a sign of things to come, the United States cast its first veto on the Security Council, the first of what would subsequently total more than 70 over the next 20 years.

The rapid growth in membership after 1960 is one of the least understood, yet nonetheless most important, phenomena of the postwar era. The Charter of the United Nations is dedicated to the principle of self-determination. This, coupled with the unstoppable desire of subject peoples everywhere for self-rule, dramatically changed first, the composition and, then, the aims and mission of the General Assembly and other UN bodies. M. E. Chamberlain argues in his work *Decolonization* that "ideas of self-determination for all peoples, President Wilson's Fourteen Points, the Atlantic Charter, the Covenant of the League of Nations and the Charter of the United Nations are regarded as creating a climate of opinion which made the possession of colonial territories, contrary to the will of the inhabitants, seem intolerable."

During the late 1950s and early 1960s, as these newly liberated peoples joined the United Nations, a sense of optimism grew that the international community would begin to address the problems of societies held back by colonialism. But rather than resolving the problems of the world, decolonization brought with it a host of new ones. The arbitrary boundaries of many colonies—often bearing little relationship to underlying cultural, societal, or linguistic patterns—frequently violated historical relationships and economic realties, slowing postcolonial progress. Years of colonial oppression, imperial social engineering, and economic exploitation would make the quest for self-determination and sovereignty crisis-plagued under even the best of circumstances. That decolonization also occurred simultaneously with the Cold War made it a crisis of enormous proportions. The East-West struggle intensified the problems of the developing world. Superpower manipulation of the process of decolonization and postcolonial societies turned the developing world into a vast playground for the Cold War ambitions of Moscow and Washington. Owing, in part, to the developed world's obsession with "security" and geopolitics, questions of development often went largely ignored. The Cold War confrontation spread to the global South with ruinous effects that persist today.

The developing nations—or the "global South"—would have to address these issues themselves. First, the Nonaligned Movement, which sought to create a bloc of states largely removed from the East-West conflict, emerged in the mid-1950s. This was followed by the establishment in 1964 of the United Nations Conference on Trade and Development (UNCTAD), which led to the creation of the Group of 77, a caucus of developing nations within the General Assembly. The developing nations' efforts to reorient international economic policy through the New International Economic Order (NIEO) in the mid-1970s arose from increasing economic and political tensions between developing and developed nations. It ultimately lost momentum as the developed nations increasingly turned toward neo-liberal economic solutions and free trade. The achievements of a number of neo-liberal Asian economies, the so-called Asian Tigers, also undermined support for Third World development schemes.

Not everyone suffered the same fate during the process of decolonization. In some cases, self-determination was achieved with deceptive ease. In Indonesia, or the Netherlands East Indies, the United Nations took up the question of decolonization with relative ease between 1947-50. But Indonesia would prove to be something of an exception, as the Netherlands cooperated with the United Nations on a number of important steps to prepare Indonesia for independence. Moreover, and perhaps most important, decolonization in the Netherlands East Indies did not immediately become entangled in the larger issues of the Cold War. As things turned out, the succeeding crises of decolonization would not be so easy and Indonesia, made a member of the UN in 1950, would be the 60th and last state admitted to the United Nations for the next five years.

The freeze on UN membership lifted in 1955, and the next few years saw a massive increase coincident with Secretary General Dag Hammarskjöld's term. He sensed the growing importance of the newly independent world, brokering the 1955 agreement that ended the membership logjam. The UN had 60 member nations at the beginning of his tenure and more than 100 at the time of his death in the Congo in 1961. His tenure also coincided with a period of significant upheaval and conflict around the world, including the Suez Crisis (1956), the Algerian war of independence (1954–1962), the crisis over Lebanon (1958), the Congo decolonization crisis (1960–1962), and a growing American involvement in Indochina. After 1955, the United Nations would turn its attention to the problems of the newly independent world, managing conflicts largely the consequence of decolonization, and addressing issues of economic development.

The Nonaligned Movement and the Transformation of the General Assembly. The rise of the nonaligned movement was motivated in part by a desire to avoid being drawn into the superpower competition. It signaled a new direction in world politics. Its growth coincided with several of the bitterest colonial conflicts, including the struggles against the French in Indochina and Algeria. Many nonaligned nations feared that their needs and interests would be subordinated to Cold War priorities. They sought therefore to draw attention to the political, economic, and developmental problems of the Third World.

From the perspective of these newly independent states, the Security Council consisted of some of the worst colonial oppressors in history, such as Britain and France. The examples set by the USSR and United States in their spheres of influence and elsewhere were not much better. For the most part, Britain and France remained completely discredited in the eyes of the decolonizing world, something neither could ever comprehend, assuming instead that their former chattels would welcome their postcolonial meddling as a well-intentioned gesture. Of the four, the Soviet Union courted the support of the developing world most aggressively, but its treatment of its satellite states, as well as many of its allies outside its sphere of interest, undermined its credibility. Nonetheless, the Soviet economic model of rapid industrialization through state planning, far removed from what many in the developing world saw as the exploitive practices of Western capitalism, initially offered to many a tantalizing alternative approach to postcolonial development.

For a time the United States sought good relations with the developing world, as evidenced by its support for the UN's efforts to halt the 1956 British-French-Israeli attempt to overthrow Nasser and take control of Egypt and the Suez Canal. But the United States, too, had revealed in places like Iran, Guatemala, Cuba, and elsewhere that it would not hesitate to undermine or overthrow governments in the developing world that it perceived as threats to its interests. The People's Republic of China also sought to become a champion of the Third World and dispatched premier Chou en-Lai to the first gathering of nonaligned nations in 1955. But mainland China would continue to be excluded from the United Nations until 1971 and would play no role in the early UN controversies over the developing world.

The nonaligned movement featured leaders from emergent nations such as India, Egypt, and Indonesia, some of them the most dynamic and charismatic figures of the postwar era such as Nasser, Tito, Nehru, and Sukarno. Meeting for the first time at Bandung, Indonesia, in 1955, delegations from 29 nonaligned nations, including six from Africa, gathered to discuss matters of common interest and concern. The Bandung conclave served as a catalyst for further cooperative efforts and subsequently resulted in the establishment of the nonaligned caucus, which became the largest caucus at the United Nations, increasing the pressure to expand its membership. In 1960 alone, seventeen newly independent states joined the UN, 16 of them from Africa. By the end of 1960 it was clear that the decolonizing world would soon be the majority in the General Assembly. Hammarskjöld's whirlwind tour of Africa that year, where he visited 21 nations, further demonstrated the growing importance of the decolonizing world.

The United Nations Conference on Trade and Development (UNCTAD) 1964.

The overall economic performance of the developing countries had been comparatively steady throughout the 1950s. By the mid-1960s, however, many developing countries became frustrated with their stagnant or diminishing economic prospects. As the initial optimism of independence faded, they confronted intractable problems of underdevelopment. Many observers have attributed their poor economic performance to colonial exploitation. In fact, imperialism and colonial economic systems had impoverished much of the world. But the immediate goals of decolonization—such as independence and the removal of alien rule—would often prove easier to attain than postcolonial economic development.

Underdevelopment stemmed, in part, from the legacy of colonial economic structures, where mercantilist systems, designed to serve the imperial core, or metropole, established colonies to obtain raw materials. The economic structures of these colonies were dysfunctional. In many cases manufacturing and industrialization were prohibited to avoid competition with metropolitan interests. The imperial powers repressed local aspirations and often refused to nurture nascent indigenous political and economic elites that might have provided a foundation for postcolonial development. This colonial economic legacy was often typified by dependency on exporting of raw materials, lack of economic diversity, and chronic underindustrialization. Such societies also suffered from insufficient sources of private capital, and corruption in both the public and private spheres. As Nobel Laureate in Economics Amartya Sen shows in his work *Development As Freedom*, these conditions often resulted in widespread poverty, few sources of government revenue, over-centralization, and inadequate systems of education, health care, and welfare. Moreover, such problems usually led to authoritarian or un-democratic forms of government, weak legal systems, and the denial of civil, human, and economic rights, particularly for women and children.

Postcolonial societies faced other hardships. Many developing nations confronted problems of geography, environment, class, caste, and tribal-ism that hampered economic development. In some cases their tradi-tional cultural practices seemed irreconcilable with economic modern-ization and global economic integration. Societal patterns common to the developing world, such as underutilization of the workforce owing to cultural restrictions on the role of women, placed further barriers to development. Traditional cultures often faced stark choices between maintaining and protecting their customs or abandoning them in the face of economic competition and modernization. In some cases any ef-fort to abandon or modify traditional practices resulted in a backlash, undermining even the most modest efforts at reform. For these reasons, and others, much of the global South ultimately proved unprepared to participate in the world economy.

These problems raised a question increasingly debated in the Gen-eral Assembly during the 1960s and 1970s: in a global economic system designed by developed nations and predicated upon the economic theory of comparative advantage—where nations would concentrate on produc-ing whatever goods gave them the greatest cost advantage—what ulti-mately happens to those nations who have little or nothing to contribute to the global economy? And what of the billions spent on the agricul-tural subsidies, and the trade barriers, of the advanced industrial na-tions? Do such practices make comparative advantage obsolete?

Many developing nations found prevailing economic doctrines inade-quate and grew more and more dissatisfied with the structure of the world economy. Some saw modern multinational corporations as instru-ments of neocolonialism, pursuing economic gains in the developing world much like the colonial exploiters. They argued that the dominant economic consensus, established at Bretton Woods in 1944 (when very few developing nations had achieved independence) largely reflected the needs and aims of the developed nations. No developing nations had been represented at Bretton Woods. Many, seeking new paths for emerging economies to navigate their way out of their economic problems, increasingly questioned the fairness of the system, arguing that it did not address their needs.

Out of this was born the United Nations Conference on Trade and Development (UNCTAD) at Geneva in the spring of 1964. UNCTAD was inspired by the nonaligned movement, arguing for more equitable terms of trade and more generous terms for financing development schemes. At least initially, some in the industrialized world sympathized, as when US President Kennedy proclaimed that the 1960s should be the development decade and the UN, with much optimism, subsequently declared its first Development Decade in 1961. In the initial euphoria of decolonization many in the developing world believed that incremental capital accumulation, coupled with steady increases in Gross National Product, would alleviate poverty and lead to prosperity in the global South. Some suggested that the developing nations could replicate the example of the developed world and avoid the trial and error of experimentation and innovation. How to achieve this was hotly debated, and no consensus indicated the best path.

Many of the newly independent nations remained dependent on exporting raw materials and agricultural products at a time when global prices for such commodities remained persistently stagnant or in decline. Meanwhile, prices of manufactured goods continued to rise, and the goal of establishing manufacturing sectors grew more distant for many. The feeling grew that the Bretton Woods system was inappropriate for the needs of developing nations. Thus began the quest for a global trade policy less detrimental to developing nations' interests. UNCTAD embodied this Third World point of view and launched a critique of international economic institutions such as the General Agreement on Tariffs and Trade (GATT), the IMF, and the World Bank.

The renowned Argentine economist Raul Prebisch became the first Secretary General of UNCTAD. He argued that the benefits of international trade were not distributed fairly between the center and the periphery and that this relationship would remain essentially exploitive and neocolonial. UNCTAD's views also received support from dependency theory, which argued that the world economic order essentially reflected the needs and interests of the advanced industrial nations. A further boost came from developmental scholarship, with works such as

Walter Rodney's *How Europe Underdeveloped Africa*, Paul Baran's *Political Economy of Growth*, Samir Amin's *Accumulation on a World Scale*, and Andre Gunder Frank's *Capitalism and Underdevelopment in Latin America*.

The Group of 77 emerged from this ferment as a Third World caucus. Organized in 1964 at the initial meeting of UNCTAD, originally consisting of 75 members, it sought to maximize the collective negotiating power of the Third World. But the influence of UNCTAD and the G-77 peaked in the late 1970s, at the very time neo-liberal economic ideology was gaining ascendancy. Increasingly, UNCTAD's mission changed. How much this was the result of failed economic policies of developing countries, how much the result of a global economic system persistently tailored to the needs of the West, how much a consequence of growing Western hostility, is open to debate.

Development Issues Become Focus of the United Nations. By the 1970s, the goals of the developing countries were changing. As UNCTAD approached its second decade, a crisis occurred as more developing nations fell short of even their most modest developmental goals. During the first decade after decolonization, the benefits of global economic growth had largely failed to trickle down to the developing nations. These failures and the worldwide economic recession of the 1970s inspired a reassessment of the goals and aims of development. Most developing nations had made little or no economic progress since independence. The declining economic performance of the Third World, the alarming emergence of the concept of an even more developmentally backward "Fourth World," and the official UN designation of Least Developed Countries (LDCs), led to a reexamination of the developing world's global economic strategies.

In 1974 the Group of 77 launched the New International Economic Order (NIEO) to promote its interests, such as the lowering of tariffs on developing nations' exports and redeployment of some the developing world's industry to the global South. The NIEO also called for reform of the international trading system, support for the nationalization of key industries, and control over excessive price and supply fluctuations of commodities and raw materials. Cultural prohibitions against educating and employing women were also increasingly seen as impediments to development. Thus, the mid-1970s also brought a growing emphasis on the role of women in economic development. Begun in 1975, the UN's Women in Development Decade, accelerated awareness of the centrality of women in developmental questions.

In the late 1970s and early 1980s, changes in the political outlook of several of the key developed nations would have an indirect impact on the developing world. By the 1980s, the terms of trade for the developing world further deteriorated. Moreover, in the West, leaders such as US President Jimmy Carter, British Prime Minister Harold Wilson, and West German Chancellor Willy Brandt, who were favorably inclined to the needs of the developing world were eventually succeeded by a group of leaders with more ideological views toward the global South, such as Ronald Reagan, Margaret Thatcher, and Helmut Kohl. These neo-liberal proponents were more circumspect about Third World interests, instead advocating laissez-faire market solutions to developmental questions. Older issues, such as the redistribution of global wealth, nationalization, and trade protection increasingly gave way to an emphasis on direct foreign investment, market standardization, and trade penetration. Furthermore, the obvious failures of the Soviet economic model, stagnating not only in the USSR but in other planned economies, further soured much of the developing world on central planning and the command economic model.

The developing world's lack of power in international politics and the increasingly divergent aims within the developing world, also contributed to the ultimate failure of Third World development efforts at the United Nations. The growing debt crisis in the developing world put many nations on the defensive. The emergence of the so-called Asian tiger economies—such as South Korea, Singapore, Hong Kong, and Taiwan—with their skilled workforces, emphasis on manufactured goods and financial services, aggressive export-oriented economies, and technological advances, seemed to offer an alternative model. To many, the Asian tigers had discovered a magic path to prosperity. How this model could be applied to other parts of the developing world with vastly different societies, cultures, histories, and geographies was less clear. The inexorable path to global market liberalization suffered some setbacks, starting with the General Agreement on Tariffs and Trade's (GATT) replacement with the more controversial World Trade Organization (WTO) and the stumbles of several of the previously showcased Asian economies in the 1990s.

As Nobel Laureate in Economics Joseph Stiglitz has argued in his work *Globalization and Its Discontents,* challenges to the Bretton Woods system and its supporting "Washington consensus" are fueling the backlash against globalization throughout the developing world. The impasse among the 148 nations of the World Trade Organization threatens to derail prospects for future global trade agreements. Talks in Seattle in 1999 and Cancun in 2003 were intended to further that process, but their failure exposed deep philosophical differences between North and South over trade liberalization.

The UN has sought to remedy many of these problems. The conflict between the established, industrialized, market economies and the less-developed ones has found an outlet at the United Nations as a venue for expressing grievances and promoting various changes in the international order. The UN also continues to devote significant resources to development. Its disbursements, including loans and grants, exceed $10 billion annually, and the United Nations Development Program (UNDP), the largest multilateral source of development grants, supports more than 5,000 projects worldwide with a budget of $1.3 billion. The World Bank alone accounts for more than $300 billion in development projects. In addition, UNICEF allocates nearly $1 billion a year on health care, nutrition, basic education, and immunization, in more than 130 developing countries.

The end of the Cold War removed some areas of conflict between the developing world and the West, but not in the economic realm. UN scholar Evan Luard has observed that the North-South conflict has been intensified as the wealth gap between them has widened. There have been some promising developments toward reconciliation between North and South, such as the European Union's recent acknowledgment of its role in aggravating the wealth gap, but wide differences of opinion persist.

Conflicts and Crises in the Developing World. The common challenges of underdevelopment often served as a bond among diverse nations in the postcolonial era. The developing world is by no means a unified bloc, however, and has in fact been plagued by numerous interstate and intrastate conflicts, many of them the persistent consequences of colonialism or the Cold War. "Many of the new states that emerged in Africa and Asia during that period were multinational," observes Robert Gregg in *About Face: The United States and the United Nations*, "frequently as the result of the artificiality of borders, which was colonialism's legacy."

Several regional conflicts with potential for destabilization are occurring in the developing world. The conflict between India and Pakistan, for example, is one of the longest running disputes in the history of the UN and, in light of those countries' testing nuclear weapons in 1998, has immense potential for regional and global destabilization. The bloody partition of British India at the time of independence in 1947 was, in part, a result of Britain botching its post-imperial strategy, a further blot on the grim legacy of British rule in South Asia. The partition, which violently tore apart numerous historic provinces, cultures, and peoples, provoked a massive refugee crisis, with nearly 20 million people displaced or forcibly relocated, and as many as 500,000 killed in widespread sectarian violence.

The consequences of partition persist to this day. India and Pakistan continue their standoff along a heavily militarized border. The outbreak of wars between them in 1947, 1965, 1971—the last resulting in a further partition of Pakistan and creating Bangladesh—underscore the fragile nature of their coexistence. The UN has sought to reduce tensions between India and Pakistan. Secretary General U Thant achieved a cease-fire during the 1965 war, but persistently heavy military spending has deterred a long-term resolution, and has undermined the development strategies of both states.

One of the most dangerous potential flash points of the India-Pakistan conflict is the disputed province of Jammu and Kashmir, with nearly 9 million people, a majority of them Muslim. At the 1947 partition of India, the ruling Maharajah of Kashmir, Hari Singh, a Hindu ruler of a predominantly Muslim state, sought to rule an independent state, but ultimately allied himself with India in October 1947 in exchange for Indian military support to fend off an incursion of Afridi tribal forces. The plebiscite the Maharajah promised to hold to determine the ultimate wishes of the peoples of Kashmir never happened. To many, India's intervention in Kashmir and its eventual annexation violated the former British Viceroy's plan to partition the subcontinent according to religion. Pakistan subsequently supported the tribal invaders and conflict continued in the province until a UN-sponsored cease-fire in 1949, followed by the establishment of a UN-enforced Line of Control partitioning Kashmir. Pakistan and India both claim Kashmir, with Pakistan controlling the northern part and India the southern part.

The dispute came before the United Nations in January 1948 and has been an item on the Security Council agenda ever since. The United Nations Military Observer Group there is the longest in continuous operation. The UN has made clear its desire for self-determination for the peoples of Kashmir, to be settled by a plebiscite, but India persists in treating the Kashmir question as an internal dispute. Pakistan has argued that India has breached several United Nations Security Council resolutions calling for a plebiscite among Kashmiris to choose rule by India or Pakistan. India accuses Pakistan of supporting terrorism in Kashmir. Pakistan denies the charge, countering that it merely supports the legitimate struggle for self-determination. Nonetheless, since the rising against Indian rule re-ignited in 1989 approximately 40,000 people have been killed in Kashmir, India's only Muslim-majority state. The conflict over Jammu and Kashmir, which has been violently revived in recent years, remains unresolved, with the potential for massive destabilization of the subcontinent, the wider Asian area, and beyond.

In East Timor, the United Nations played an active role organizing a plebiscite, dispatching peacekeepers, and overseeing a multistep process toward independence. East Timor had been a Portuguese colony since 1566. After its independence was declared in 1975, a brief civil war resulted in the victory of the Revolutionary Front for an Independent East Timor. The new regime initiated policies of land reform and literacy, which were halted by Indonesia's invasion at the end of 1975. The Indonesian President, General Suharto, had come to power with Western backing in a 1965 coup overthrowing the popular independence leader Sukarno. Suharto shared with the US a fear that the post-independence government in East Timor had the potential to become an outpost for international communism in Asia. Because Suharto was an important strategic ally in the Cold War, the West materially aided his regime, even as Indonesia ruled East Timor through violence and intimidation, with frequent human rights abuses. Indonesian rule was marked by widespread torture and the murder of a large portion of the population.

Suharto's regime grew more repressive, despotic, and corrupt, and the end of the Cold War removed many of the rationales for supporting him. During the devastating Asian economic crisis of the 1990s Suharto's kleptocratic regime disintegrated, leading to UN-sponsored talks over the status of East Timor, and the establishment of the United Nations Mission to the disputed province in June 1999. The mission organized a referendum on the question of independence in East Timor, which produced an overwhelming majority for independence. Violence soon resulted and the Security Council authorized a multinational force, INTERFET, to East Timor in September 1999. (*See Document No. 14.*) After restoring order and establishing an interim administration, the UN oversaw the departure of Indonesian forces, supervised the first parliamentary elections, and facilitated the declaration of East Timorese independence on May 20, 2002.

CHAPTER 4

THE UNITED NATIONS AND
THE MIDDLE EAST

The United Nations and the Arab-Israeli Dispute.
Throughout its history, the United Nations has played substantial roles
in numerous controversies in the Middle East. Among the most important are the questions of Palestine and the Arab-Israeli dispute, which
the UN played a key role in determining the partition plan of 1947 that
led to the creation of the state of Israel. The UN also dispatched small
peacekeeping and observer missions to the Sinai Peninsula, Gaza, Lebanon, and the Golan Heights. It played a large part in the refugee crisis
that occurred in the aftermath of the first Arab-Israeli war and it continues humanitarian relief efforts in the occupied territories. The UN
has also passed a series of Security Council resolutions that serve as a
loose framework in the search for a settlement between Israel and the
neighboring Arab states and, later, Israel and the Palestinians.

The controversy over Palestine shared numerous commonalities with
other crises the UN has been involved with in the Middle East such as
Iraq and Lebanon. All are partial consequences of imperial contact and
colonial social engineering. The flawed mandates in Palestine, Lebanon,
and Iraq had a profound impact on their later evolution, as did the problematic application of the concept of the nation state, creating artificial
boundaries with no historical, ethnic, or religious basis. Most of the
countries in the region are not the natural and historical products of
time and space, but rather configurations arrived at arbitrarily by external powers. Moreover, the ongoing Western interest in the region's resources—particularly oil—has had a major impact on political developments.

Few places have been as affected by their recent history as Palestine
and few regions have been so profoundly affected by imperial contact.
From the vantage point of today's crisis, the most important historical
events in the region occurred in the last century. The origins of the current problem lay, not unlike other longstanding UN concerns such as
Cyprus or the India-Pakistan conflict, in the failed imperial policies of
Britain, which were decisive in determining Palestine's fate. Like Cyprus and India-Pakistan, the mishandling of the decolonization process

created problems which continue to plague the region, and the UN, to this day.

Under the Ottoman Empire, Palestine was divided into three distinct provinces, and the religious composition of the region, according to Israeli historian Avi Shlaim, author of *The Iron Wall: Israel and the Arab World*, was estimated to be approximately 80 percent Muslim Arab, 10 percent Christian Arab, and less than 10 percent Jewish. Even prior to the establishment of the British mandate for Palestine, British proclamations about the fate of the region had seriously muddied the situation. Early in the First World War the McMahon-Hussein notes of 1915–16 lured regional Arab factions into an alliance with British imperial forces to end the Ottoman Empire's rule. The Arabs seized upon the tantalizing hints the British made that, once rid of the Ottomans, the Arabs would achieve self-rule in the region. The subsequent Sykes-Picot agreement of 1916 contradicted much of the spirit of McMahon-Hussein, laying instead the groundwork for an Anglo-French partition of the region after the war. Moreover, the British-issued Balfour Declaration of 1917 expressed support for a Jewish homeland in Palestine. These latter proclamations marked a radical departure for Palestine. The British consolidated their hold on the region under a League of Nations mandate, and Palestine became increasingly important to British imperial aims as a gateway to the Iraqi oil fields through Transjordan and for its strategic location near the Suez Canal. The British allowed substantial Jewish migration to the region, fueling a demographic revolution in Palestine which provoked unrest and periodic resistance of the Arab population. In the late 1930s, in the hope of calming Palestine, the British halted Jewish immigration at the very time that the increasingly perilous plight of European Jews made the refugee situation most urgent.

As Tom Segev has explained in *One Palestine, Complete: Jews and Arabs Under the British Mandate*, the British sought to hold on to Palestine after the Second World War for strategic purposes. But the war's consequences—and particularly the killing of six million European Jews in the Holocaust—decisively determined Palestine's postwar fate. Sympathy for the Jewish people created worldwide political support, not only for higher levels of immigration, but also for some sort of a Jewish state. Meanwhile, Britain's hold on Palestine was becoming increasingly tenuous. Years of violent struggle culminated in the murder of much of the British High Commission during the bombing of Jerusalem's King David Hotel by the Jewish ultranationalist organization, Irgun, in 1947.

The British then feebly submitted the Palestine question to the United Nations without having done anything to prepare for what should become of the region.

The Palestine crisis and its aftermath would become one of the UN's longest-running disputes. The United Nations Special Committee on Palestine (UNSCOP) was established in April 1947 to seek a resolution satisfactory to both sides. UNSCOP issued majority and minority reports. The majority recommendations (*see Document No. 15*) suggested partitioning Palestine into two separate states, one Jewish and one Arab; the minority report recommended a federated unitary state consisting of Jews and Arabs coexisting. Both supported the idea of placing Jerusalem under international status. The Jewish Agency for Palestine accepted the plan, but the Palestine Arab Higher Committee rejected it, as did neighboring Arab states.

In November 1947 the partition plan was incorporated into General Assembly Resolution 181. (*See document No. 16.*) When the British relinquished their mandate on May 14, 1948, the state of Israel was proclaimed. In the ensuing conflict, first with the Palestinian Arabs and then with neighboring Arab states, Israel gained much of the territory demarcated for the Arab population. The United Nations sought to achieve an armistice, but its mediator, Folke Bernadotte of Sweden, was assassinated by Israeli ultranationalists in September 1948. In the aftermath of the 1948–1949 war, the United Nations faced a massive refugee crisis in and around Palestine. General Assembly Resolution 194 called for the settlement or compensation of Palestinian refugees, and the UN set about creating the UN Relief and Works Agency for Palestine Refugees in the Near East (UNRWA), which sought to aid an estimated 700,000 refugees. UNRWA established 50 camps throughout the region in the West Bank, Gaza, Jordan, Lebanon, and Syria. Today, nearly six decades later, an estimated 4 million Palestinian refugees are registered with UNRWA.

The United Nations has also worked to guide the peace process in the Middle East through the passage of resolutions. In the aftermath of the 1967 war, in which Israel captured large portions of Jordan, Egypt, and Syria, the Security Council passed Resolution 242 (*see Document No. 17*), underscoring that territories acquired by war cannot be kept indefinitely. This Resolution became the basis of land-for-peace initiatives leading to the Camp David accords of 1979, the Madrid peace initiative of 1991, the Oslo accords of 1993 and the (ultimately failed) bids for a settlement during Camp David II and at Sharm al-Sheik in 2000–2001. Beyond Resolution 242, the events of 1967 have had profound consequences for the region. Since the 1967 war, Israeli foreign and domestic policy has become increasingly focused on the fate of the Palestinians and the ultimate disposition of the occupied territories, where thousands of Israelis have settled in the past three decades. International opinion has also focused on the fate of the Palestinians since 1967 and the membership of the General Assembly has grown increasingly hostile to Israel, passing, for example, the controversial 1975 Resolution equating Zionism with racism. (*See Document No. 18.*) Yet the Israeli-Palestinian dispute—a potentially explosive issue with broader regional and international implications—continues unabated. Successive Israeli governments remain committed to excluding the UN from the search for a resolution to the conflict. The Palestinian cause, long an emotional issue in Middle East politics, has gained increasing recognition in Europe and the United States in recent years, particularly since the Oslo peace accords of 1993. Meanwhile, Israel finds itself increasingly isolated and under siege, while the Palestinians have grown more desperate, subsisting in substandard communities and refugee camps, their aspirations for self-determination thwarted generation after generation. The ongoing carnage of the conflict demonstrates how violence and vengeance perpetuate each other in an endless, circular, dispiriting progression. Yet it remains doubtful that the United Nations can play a greater role in the conflict anytime soon.

The Suez Crisis and the United Nations, 1956. The Suez crisis of 1956 also drew the United Nations into the region. The UN sought to halt the Anglo-French-Israeli invasion of Egypt and provided substantial peacekeeping forces in what Stanley Meisler has called "one of the most spectacular single achievements of the U.N. during its first fifty years." The dispute over Egyptian leader Abdel Gamel Nasser's nationalization of the Suez Canal was essentially a war of decolonization. It should be seen in the context of Britain's loss of India and Palestine and its ongoing colonial war in Malaya, as well as French losses of Syria, Lebanon and Indochina and its ongoing colonial war in Algeria. The two colonial powers saw Egypt as an opportunity to take a stand against their diminishing imperial status in the world.

The Suez Canal opened in 1869 and reinforced the strategic and economic importance of Egypt as a lifeline to Britain's colonies in Asia and the Pacific. Western commercial interests in Egypt expanded in the late nineteenth century. Britain came to dominate Egypt through "informal" imperialism, interfering in Egyptian affairs with impunity, installing ruling elites favorable to British imperial aims, and maneuvering to keep less sympathetic factions out of power. The British regularly used massive force and violence to crush Egyptian resistance and aspirations.

In the wake of a 1952 coup overthrowing the pro-Western monarchy and proclaiming a republic, Nasser emerged as the absolute leader of a Free Officers Movement. He embarked upon a moderate political course, initially looking to the United States as a prospective ally, and simultaneously challenging Western influence in the region. The Western powers had been creating a Cold War alliance—or "northern tier"—of states in the region running from Turkey, through Iraq, Iran, and Pakistan, which came to be known as the Baghdad Pact. In part because of his anticolonial feelings, particularly toward British imperial power, Nasser had little enthusiasm for such a pact, which would once again place Egypt at the service of Western interests in the region. Instead, he increasingly moved into the nonaligned orbit, attending the 1955 summit in Bandung, Indonesia, along with Nehru, Sukarno, and Tito.

After a series of Western diplomatic blunders and misunderstandings over Egypt, Nasser nationalized the Suez Canal on July 26, 1956. In response, during the autumn of 1956, the British, French, and Israeli governments colluded in secret to invade Egypt and overthrow Nasser. They launched an attack on October 29 when Israel invaded the Sinai. In what many have called Hammarskjöld's finest hour, the United Nations held its first ever emergency session of the General Assembly. Under the Uniting for Peace precedent the General Assembly passed a Resolution, 997 (*see Document No. 19*), supported by both Washington and Moscow, aiming to pressure Britain and France into a cease-fire. Under Hammarskjöld's leadership, the General Assembly subsequently mounted a large multinational peacekeeping operation, in some ways a model for future peacekeeping efforts, which by 1957 totaled 6,000 troops. UN forces supervised a cease-fire, oversaw the withdrawal of British, French, and Israeli forces from Egypt, and worked to maintain stability on the tense Israeli-Egyptian frontier.

The legacies and consequences of Suez were many. Nasser's defiance of the West inspired anticolonial aspirations everywhere. His prestige was never higher than after Suez, as Syria, and later North Yemen, joined with Egypt to form the short-lived United Arab Republic (1958–61). In the aftermath of Suez, a violent coup in Iraq swept away the pro-Western Hashemite monarchy in 1958, owing, in part, to the political aftershocks of the Suez crisis. Also, in 1958, both the United Nations and the United States became involved in Lebanon, partly to prevent any further triumphs for Nasserism in the region.

The United Nations in the Broader Middle East. The UN has also been active in a series of crises in Lebanon, Iran, and Yemen. Lebanon has been a place of intense United Nations involvement. It first intervened in 1958 and there again in 1978. Lebanon had inherent instabilities as a result of the artificial and arbitrary nature of its origins. While under League mandate, the French created Lebanon —or *Grand Liban*—along religious lines chiefly to serve their imperial interests in the region. They ruled it for a quarter century. The French imperial creation of this colonial entity, dominated by the Maronite Christian community, ultimately led to the annexation of several surrounding, predominantly Muslim, territories to create a viable state. The populations within those annexed areas were never consulted, and broader Lebanese aspirations were constantly thwarted by French imperial aims in the region. (The French also controlled neighboring Syria under a League of Nations mandate.) According to Robert Fisk, author of *Pity the Nation: The Abduction of Lebanon*, the French manipulated the various religious groups in Lebanon to maximize their imperial control. The Maronites remained a minority within the Lebanese state, but the French sought to ensure their domination of the political system. Many of the problems of Lebanon, particularly the bloody civil war that wracked the country from 1975 to 1990, are the result of the inherent instability of the Lebanese state structure owing, in part, to these French machinations.

Following the failed Anglo-French-Israeli invasion of Egypt in 1956, the Arab world grew increasingly anti-Western. Lebanon, with its conservative Maronite Christian government and strong identification with Western interests, grew increasingly isolated in the region. The creation of Nasser's United Arab Republic (UAR) heightened Arab nationalism in Lebanon and neighboring Arab states, inspiring the revolution in Iraq in 1958. That same year Lebanon lodged a complaint with the United Nations that its border with Syria had been breached. Syria, which had controlled Lebanon long before the arrival of the French, had only recently joined with Egypt in the creation of the UAR. Thereafter the politics of the Arab Middle East were increasingly fracturing among Nasserites, Hashemites, and the Saudis. US Marines were subsequently dispatched to Lebanon under the newly proclaimed Eisenhower Doctrine and, in June, the Security Council dispatched a military observer group. Secretary General Hammarskjöld negotiated with neighboring Arab states a pledge of noninterference in Lebanon. Both US and UN forces withdrew by the end of the year.

A second crisis erupted in 1975 when fierce fighting broke out between the Lebanese Christian Phalange militia and the Palestine Liberation Organization (PLO), which had moved into Lebanon after having been forced out of Jordan in 1970. The Phalange-Palestinian conflict sparked the Lebanese civil war, which lasted 15 years. It took 150,000 lives, most of them civilians, and provoked Syrian (1976) and Israeli (1978, 1982) invasions. When Israel, claiming its border with Lebanon was threatened, invaded Lebanon in March 1978, the United Nations launched its most extensive operation in the region. The United Nations Interim Forces in Lebanon (UNIFIL) sought to facilitate the Israeli withdrawal and aid the Lebanese government in reestablishing order. The UN negotiated the withdrawal of Israeli forces by June 1978, but both Israel and the PLO left behind proxies to carry on the war, which continued to destabilize the Lebanese state as well as the border area between Lebanon and Israel. The UN's Interim Forces remained in Lebanon for two decades.

The 1982 Israeli move into Lebanon came on the heels of the Security Council calling for a cease-fire along the Israeli-Lebanese border. Israeli forces, allied with the Lebanese Christian Phalange movement, followed a plan drafted by Minister of Defense Ariel Sharon, and drove all the way to Beirut within days. This provoked further chaos, resulting in the massacre by Phalange militia of some 700 Palestinian refugees at the Sabra and Shatila refugee camps. It also brought about a US intervention that came to grief in Beirut where hundreds of US Marines died. Israeli forces remained in Lebanon for more than a decade with significant losses of life on all sides. While the fighting over Lebanon has calmed significantly in recent years with the establishment of a Syrian protectorate over the region, the intense suffering of the Lebanese people, and their anger at the international community, make it a potential flashpoint in the region. The various interventions in Lebanon, and the UN's inability to stem the violence, have had lasting consequences to this day for the broader Middle East.

Iran, too, has been subjected to the whims of imperial powers. Perhaps inevitably, the United Nations has also been involved there on a number of occasions. First, in 1946, the UN sought to facilitate the withdrawal of Soviet troops from northern Iran in the very first dispute taken up by the Security Council. After four months of negotiations, Soviet forces withdrew. Several years later, in May 1951, the International Court of Justice took up the question of the nationalization of British-owned oil properties when Muhammad Mossaddeq's nationalized the Anglo-Iranian Oil Company. As told by Stephen Kinzer in *All the Shah's Men: A Middle East Coup and the Roots of Middle East Terror*, Mossaddeq was overthrown by an Anglo-American covert operation in 1953, before the UN could comprehensively address the matter. This restored the exiled Shah to power and resumed the flow of oil on terms favorable to Western interests.

A quarter of a century later, after years of growing discontent throughout Iran with the pro-Western regime, the Shah was overthrown by an Islamic revolution led by the Shia cleric, the Ayatollah Ruhollah Musavi Khomeini. Persistent resentment of foreign interference in Iranian affairs contributed to the Shah's overthrow. A group of militant supporters of the revolution seized the US embassy in Teheran in 1979 and held the embassy staff for more than a year. Iran was condemned by the Security Council, the General Assembly, and the International Court of Justice for so blatantly breaching international law. Iran became a pariah state in the international community, with important consequences owing to the West's muted reaction to Iraqi President Saddam Hussein's unprovoked invasion of Iran in 1980. Iran once again became the main focus of the United Nations as the Secretary General's office and the Security Council sought some resolution of the Iran-Iraq conflict (1980-1988).

The United Nations also played a role in North Yemen, where civil war had broken out in 1962, evolving into a struggle between Nasserism, which was backing the Yemeni republican forces, and the Saudis, who supported the Yemeni royal family. UN Secretary General U Thant sought to remove forces of the United Arab Republic and halt Saudi aid. The UN dispatched an observer mission in 1963. They certified the disengagement between Saudi Arabia and the United Arab Republic, and the mission terminated in 1964 after Egypt and Saudi Arabia agreed to end their support for the various factions there.

The United Nations and Iraq. The United Nations, and particularly the Security Council, has loomed large in the multiple crises involving Iraq. In fact, in recent years few matters have so engaged the United Nations as Iraq, an issue that has dominated the Security Council agenda since 1990. Beyond the initial resolutions condemning Iraq's attack on Kuwait in 1990 and calling for a withdrawal from the tiny emirate, the UN has become involved in humanitarian and refugee issues in and around Iraq. It monitored borders, established so-called "no-fly zones" over Iraq, enforced economic sanctions, and conducted weapons inspections. In retrospect, Iraq has been the focus of one of the UN's most remarkable moments when, as the Cold War was winding down in 1990, the Security Council obtained approval for a multinational force to remove Iraq from Kuwait in early 1991. Yet Iraq is also the setting for one of the Security Council's greatest failures: the Anglo-American dismissal of the reservations of the other members of the Security Council and launching of a war in Iraq in the spring of 2003.

Despite the attention Iraq has received in the West since 1990, its history, and particularly the way that history has conditioned and shaped its destiny, remains relatively unknown—this despite the emergence of much remarkable scholarship in the last decade. As Timothy J. Paris has shown in *Britain, the Hashemites and Arab Rule*, Iraq shares much with other Middle East trouble spots that have concerned the United Nations such as Palestine and Lebanon. Like those areas, many of Iraq's contemporary problems are largely attributable to its experience under European mandate. Comprised of three distinct Ottoman provinces of Basra, Baghdad, and Mosul, during the First World War declarations by the British raised expectations that local Arab factions would achieve self-government in the area. Upon such promises—such as the infamous McMahon-Hussein notes of 1915–1916—many regional Arab factions fought with the British empire against Ottoman forces in the region. Britain had other designs for the region and desired to rule Mesopotamia directly. The British reneged on the promises to the Arabs, seeking instead an Anglo-French partition of the Middle East and a division of spoils under the 1916 Sykes-Picot Agreement. Revelation of this secret agreement caused consternation among the Arabs as well as long-term bitterness. The British ultimately had to consent to a League of Nations mandate for the area, with themselves as the mandatory power for what would subsequently become Iraq. This did nothing to assuage the Arab sense of betrayal. As John Keay has established in his work, *Sowing the Wind: the Seeds of Conflict in the Middle East*, Iraq's problems were intensified by the widespread social and demographic engineering that occurred under the British mandate. Iraq's arbitrary borders in no way reflected underlying cultural patterns or historical relationships. The artificial assembly of this nascent state was reinforced by the British imperial effort to manufacture a ruling elite from the minority Sunni population, installing as King the formerly Arabian-based Hashemite princeling Feisal ibn Hussein al Hashem in 1921, following a plebiscite of dubious credibility.

While the Sunni minority was promoted by the British, the new state remained predominantly Shia, with a substantial Kurdish minority. Both of these peoples were largely excluded from participation in the running of the state by the British-imposed governing elite. The British empire sought to protect its interests without regard for local aspirations, making the situation much worse than it otherwise might have been. The British role in Iraq was traditionally imperial. They backed a friendly elite, the Hashemites, to promote British imperial aims in the region and favored the Sunni minority. London also secured long-term contracts, on highly favorable terms, for the extraction of Iraq's oil. It also sought to secure Iraq as a strategic outpost in the region, maintaining British bases with substantial forces, and terrorizing the civilian population with aerial bombardment at the slightest sign of resistance. As Toby Dodge has shown in his work *Inventing Iraq: The Failure of Nation Building and a History Denied*, the peoples who inhabited Iraq were never passive bystanders. With false British promises of independence still fresh, there were numerous acts of resistance against British imperial power, which had alienated the growing urban, educated, middle class and poisoned the political climate.

The mandate formally ended in 1932, but the British saw Iraq as part of their informal empire. They maintained bases to support their frequent interventions into Iraqi political life and to secure their economic interests. Charles Tripp, in *A History of Iraq*, sees the British mandate as "a troubling legacy which the grant of formal independence did little to remove." Despite the termination of the mandate, many Iraqis continued to resist British imperial domination of Iraqi life and politics. Post-mandate Iraqi history is marked by numerous uprisings and acts of resistance against British imperial power and its Hashemite allies. The culmination was the 1958 coup which overthrew the pro-Western ruling elite. With this history in mind, Iraq has remained highly sensitive to outside interference or exploitation of any kind to this day.

In 1980, without any previous warning, Iraq attacked neighboring Iran, the latter at the time a pariah state because of the continuing hostage crisis. The international response was downplayed. Iraq was clearly the aggressor, but the United States and a number of regional states tilted in favor of Iraq and offered various sorts of support and indirect aid. The United Nations worked to resolve the Iran-Iraq War, ultimately leading to acceptance on both sides of Security Council Resolution 598 in 1988, which produced a truce and the dispatch of an observer mission to monitor the border. But the human toll of the war was staggering, with total losses, almost equally shared, at an estimated 400,000 lives. Moreover, that Iraq had attacked Iran without provocation and without suffering the sanction of the United Nations for having done so, was never seriously addressed by the international community. The lesson was not lost on the Iraqi leader, Saddam Hussein.

Iraq earned the gratitude of the West for its aggression against Iran. Yet two years later, Iraq would be at the center of the world's attention, and in the cross hairs of Western condemnation, for its invasion and annexation of neighboring oil-rich and, perhaps most important, pro-Western Kuwait. Iraq's complex relations with Kuwait are rooted in regional history. Iraq long nurtured grievances against the emirate, charging that it had sought to illegally extract oil from under Iraqi borders and claiming Kuwait as its 19th province. "Although there were long-standing disagreements between Iraq and Kuwait" notes Gareth Evans, "there were no real attempts to resolve them. Failure to resolve this issue earlier led to later problems." Saddam Hussein mistakenly assumed the West would not oppose his 1990 invasion. In fact, the Iraqi leader had received very confused signals from Western officials— including the US ambassador—in the months preceding the attack. Nonetheless, on August 2, 1990 more than 150,000 Iraqi troops invaded Kuwait and chased the ruling al-Sabah clan into exile.

The UN role in the 1990–91 Gulf Crisis must be seen in the context of the ending of the Cold War. The decline of superpower competition —worldwide, regionally, and at the United Nations—meant that the Security Council could serve as a forum for resolutions and subsequent action against Iraq. "The easing of Cold War tensions, more than anything else," argues Robert Gregg, "created the conditions in which Security Council agreement on the response to Iraq's invasion of Kuwait was possible." The Security Council passed 29 resolutions against Iraq, the most significant—Security Council Resolutions 660 and 678—(*see Documents No. 20 and 21*) authorizing the possible use of force against Iraq, the first time the Security Council had approved such a measure since the Korean War.

The combined air and ground operations against Iraq concluded in weeks. After the cessation of hostilities, Iraq accepted all UN resolutions passed since August 1990. In the post-Gulf War years the Security Council passed another 30 resolutions regarding Iraq, the most important establishing a truce observation mission, monitoring the border, and supervising a sanctions regime. Furthermore, a United Nations Special Commission (UNSCOM) was created by Security Council Resolution 687 to inspect and supervise the destruction of Iraq's weapons programs. The Gulf War had numerous consequences for the region, many not anticipated at the time. It led to a US military garrison in the neighboring state of Saudi Arabia, considered by many the guardian of the holiest sites in Islam, which was soon to fuel outrage throughout much of the region.

The second Iraq crisis (2002-) unfolded in several substantially different ways from the first and would have vastly different consequences, both for the UN and the world, most of them not yet fully understood. First, as Dilip Hiro has observed in *Iraq: In the Eye of the Storm*, it occurred in the context of post-September 11, when the United States developed a new national security strategy. It sought to justify preemptive attacks in the name of self-defense, contrary to Article 51 of the UN Charter, which permits the use of force only in self-defense after an attack on a member nation. The second Iraq war also lacked the clear provocation of August 1990, as well as the widespread support of the international community. Washington gave as one pretext for the war the alleged Iraqi development of weapons of mass destruction, and a subsequent Resolution, UNSCR 1441 (*see Document No. 22*), was pushed by the British and Americans in the hope of securing UN support for an invasion. The first Iraq crisis had created a sense of optimism, even euphoria, that the United Nations might emerge at the center of a new international order. The second Iraq war left many with the feeling that the United Nations, and particularly the Security Council, had been seriously undermined by the Anglo-American decision to launch a Middle

East war contrary to the wishes of other members of the Council and a majority of the members of the General Assembly, many of whom believed the crisis lacked the clarity of the previous war against Iraq and that the UN weapons inspectors had not discovered sufficient evidence to justify an attack.

Three weeks after the invasion of Iraq, Coalition forces declared victory in April 2003. But it was by no means clear what the ultimate fate of Iraq would be. Washington initially limited the UN role in Iraq and pressed ahead with its own plans to pacify the region and its restive populations. But, in the face of continuing resistance and civil chaos throughout Iraq (reminiscent of the resistance to British imperial power during and after the mandate), the US appealed for a more proactive role for the UN. The appeal was seriously questioned when in August 2003 a car bomb destroyed UN headquarters in Iraq. Included among the many dead was Sergio Vieira de Mello, the head of mission. By the middle of 2004 the UN appeared poised to play an expanded role in Iraq, as the US tentatively dropped much of its opposition and began to embrace a UN-sponsored effort to internationalize the Iraq crisis and hand over power to the Iraqi people.

CHAPTER 5

THE UNITED NATIONS AND AFRICA

Decolonization and the Quest for Self-Determination in Africa. To the casual observer, the United Nations and Africa seem made for each other. African representatives to the UN constitute the largest bloc from any continent, and African matters have engaged the UN more than any other region. The UN's focus on Africa grew parallel to the process of decolonization. Prior to 1960 the UN played almost no role in sub-Saharan black Africa. There were only four members from the region: Liberia, Ethiopia, Ghana, and Guinea. After 1960, increased African representation enlarged the General Assembly. By 1965 it included 29 members from sub-Saharan black Africa. Africa would be the United Nations' major area of involvement in the decades after 1960. There were ample reasons for this, such as the long-term problems stemming from colonial domination, the complicated nature of decolonization, persistent underdevelopment throughout much of the region, the devastating consequences of the Cold War, and the fragility of postcolonial state institutions.

The ravages of the slave trade and imperial brutality and exploitation contributed to Africa's postcolonial crisis on a number of levels. The European occupation was as brutal an example of imperial violence that one is likely to find. The colonial powers often ruled Africa through the harshest means, employing strategies of enslavement, economic exploitation, social engineering and genocide, not always practiced in other parts of their global empires.

Institutionalized violence became integral to the process of human exploitation and resource extraction employed by the European powers and their white settlement colonies. Forced labor and the destruction of indigenous societies became commonplace in the quest for riches and arable land. To enhance their power, the Europeans created exploitive hierarchical social systems. Seeking total control over their colonies Europeans encouraged a rigid ethnic classification among Africa's many peoples. These exploitive systems of domination, control, and categorization persisted long after decolonization, saddling many postcolonial regimes with institutionalized systems of repression. Many postcolonial

African states merely maintained the exploitive legacies established by colonialism.

Decolonization came relatively late to most of sub-Saharan Africa. By contrast, much of Asia and the Middle East had already enjoyed at least a decade of independence when most of Africa began to emerge from colonial domination. By the time such change swept through black Africa, the European powers had abandoned many of their colonial enterprises elsewhere. In Asia or the Middle East, for example, the Europeans departed after many decades of repressing well-organized indigenous societies and political elites. In Africa, by contrast, European colonial power often began to recede before the emergence of organized indigenous political movements. In many areas the resulting postcolonial chaos occurred because the European powers did little or nothing to prepare the local populations for independence. Furthermore, European contact often intensified African problems, leaving behind legacies of arbitrary borders, underdeveloped infrastructure, artificial social systems, economic exploitation, ethnic and racial divisions, and overdependence on the production of raw materials.

At the time of African decolonization, the Cold War had been thoroughly globalized. Other areas of decolonization, such as south Asia and the Middle East, might, at times, avoid the geopolitics of the Cold War. In Africa, the process frequently became entangled with the polarizing East-West conflict, contributing to the already heavy burdens of the postcolonial experience. Considering the violence with which Europeans pursued their colonial aims in Africa, and the meager benefits Africans gained from contact with Europe, decolonization would have been difficult under the best of circumstances. That much of Africa became a focus of superpower competition shortly after independence further aggravated an already difficult process of decolonization and state building.

Postcolonial Africa desperately needed investment, development assistance, relief from poverty and famine, educational reform, health care, and support for emerging institutions of self-government. The outside world, when taking notice of Africa at all, was more interested in geopolitical gains and securing and extracting Africa's resources. Africa most needed international support for economic development and democratization. Instead, the world took an increasingly narrow ideological view of its problems, seeking Cold War geopolitical advantage at every turn. Important opportunities were lost to Africans, but also to the wider world, which would have benefited from African development and stability.

In Africa the United Nations faced some of its toughest challenges and endured several stunning failures. The UN struggled with the harsh realities of colonial underdevelopment and exploitation. Beginning in 1960, in the former Belgian Congo, the UN embarked upon a massive, unprecedented, peacekeeping effort. This occurred in a context of heightened Cold War tensions, amidst nonexistent state institutions, in the face of a violent, unforgiving, secessionist crisis, and a predatory former colonial overseer. In South Africa, Rhodesia, and Namibia, the United Nations confronted the legacy of white colonial settlement and the dramatic struggle for self-determination during decades of white minority rule and Cold War politics. In Angola and Mozambique, the UN faced the challenge of reconstituting societies torn apart by the Cold War. In Somalia, the UN sought to respond to a massive humanitarian crisis, but soon confronted the limitations of peacekeeping and nation building as Somali civil institutions disintegrated. In Rwanda, perhaps the UN's greatest failure to date, the international community's passive response, resulted in the genocidal murder of an estimated 800,000 people, shattering the UN's credibility in the process. And, finally, in the Great Lakes region of Africa, the unhappy precedents of the Congo, Somalia, and Rwanda muted an international response to a crisis involving multiple states that resulted in the deaths of as many as 2 million people— one of the worst disasters since World War II.

Crisis in the Congo Embroils the United Nations. As the third largest country in Africa, strategically located in the middle of the continent, bordering nine other nation-states, the Congo, during its short history as an independent state, has twice been a United Nations concern. The UN's 1960–1964 intervention became a major test of so-called "first-generation" peacekeeping, one of the earliest and most complex, and certainly one of the largest, challenges the UN faced over decolonization. In retrospect, the first Congo intervention confronted the UN with insurmountable challenges, leading to the death of its most respected Secretary General. It also led to a financial crisis at the UN from which it never fully recovered. Although not perceived at the time, the Congo crisis became an important turning point in "first-generation" peacekeeping. Never again, in the three decades remaining of the Cold War, would the UN mount an operation on such a scale.

At the Congress of Berlin in 1885, at the height of the so-called scramble for Africa, King Leopold of the Belgians obtained the Congo as a personal estate. As Adam Hochschild has shown in *King Leopold's Ghost*, Belgium's domination of the Congo was harsh, even by the merciless standards of European rule in Africa. The Belgians imposed a system of forced labor using genocide and systematic terrorism to maximize the extraction of the Congo's wealth in gold, diamonds, lumber, and coffee. The modern history of the Congo cannot be understood without reference to this legacy. The well-being of the indigenous populations of the region was irrelevant and colonialism utterly failed to prepare the Congo for eventual independence and self-rule. The Belgians repressed the emergence of an indigenous colonial elite, fearing it might challenge their colonial domination. They even hoped to wield influence in the postcolonial state after independence. Beyond the obvious lack of economic or political development, the Congo remained at independence little more than a large conceptualized state, more a collection of unintegrated ethnically diverse regions than anything even remotely resembling a nation.

The Congo nevertheless became independent on June 30, 1960 but, with so little done to prepare the path to independence, the prospects for its postcolonial future remained bleak. When the new Congolese Army rose against its Belgian officers a week later, Brussels swiftly dispatched 10,000 Belgian paratroopers. This was so similar to the Anglo-French intervention in Egypt in 1956 that many suspected it had been planned well in advance as part of Belgium's neocolonial strategy. Within days, the secessionist leader Moise Tshombe, backed by Belgian mercenaries and supported by Belgian-owned mining companies, declared the independence of the resource-rich Katanga province.

The Congo's first and, as it would turn out, only democratically elected leader, Patrice Lumumba, appealed to the United Nations for assistance. Secretary General Dag Hammarskjöld invoked Article 99 of the United Nations Charter, granting him power to bring to the attention of the Security Council "any matter which in his opinion may threaten the maintenance of international peace and security." The Security Council called upon Belgium to remove its troops and, at the request of Lumumba, Hammarskjöld launched the United Nations Operation in the Congo (know by the French acronym ONUC) to keep the peace and restore order. The UN peacekeeping mission soon grew into a large multinational force of 20,000, but disagreement mounted between Lumumba and Hammarskjöld. The Secretary General, seeking to remain within the mission's mandate, sought to emphasize the maintenance of peace and avoid having the UN play an overtly partisan role. The Congolese Prime Minister, his leadership increasingly under duress, saw Hammarskjöld as too responsive to Western economic and Cold War objectives in the Congo and not sufficiently interested in the removal of the Belgians or the secession of Katanga.

Lumumba's position became increasingly difficult after he split with his erstwhile counterpart, President Joseph Kasavubu, and was placed under house arrest, under UN protection, by Army Chief of Staff Joseph Mobutu. In New York, Hammarskjöld faced his own crisis, perhaps the greatest of his tenure. In the midst of the Congo crisis, the USSR became increasingly contentious on the Security Council. The General Assembly held an emergency session on the Congo, and the Soviet Union subsequently withheld a portion of its UN dues. Soviet representatives also called for the removal of the Secretary General and his replacement with a committee of three, or *troika*. Hammarskjöld's woes mounted when Lumumba, growing more dubious of the UN's ability to protect him, fled his compound in the capital, Leopoldville (Kinsasha). The Prime Minister was subsequently captured by forces loyal to General Mobutu. Brutally tortured throughout the ordeal, Lumumba was transferred to Katanga province. There he, and several associates, were murdered, their bodies hacked to pieces and soaked in acid. Lumumba, only 35 at the time of his murder, his nation less than seven months old, would become a legend (and also, perhaps, a cautionary tale) to Third World nationalists everywhere.

Hammarskjöld faced mounting criticism in the aftermath of Lumumba's murder, further disintegration of state institutions, and the emergence of multiple factions laying claim to civil authority. In response, he announced that United Nations peacekeepers would remove the Belgians by force, if necessary. But the Secretary General, now deeply absorbed in the crisis in the Congo, lost his life in September 1961 when his plane crashed en route to a meeting with the Katangan secessionists.

The United Nations peacekeepers departed the Congo in 1964, leaving behind a fractured nation increasingly dominated by the brutal kleptocratic regime of General Mobutu. He continued the Belgian model of exploitation and repression. For the next three decades, he also provided the West with the Congo's resources and was an important Cold

War ally in strategic central Africa. The Congo debacle revealed the ease with which UN operations could be hijacked by the politics of the Cold War and called into question the effectiveness of peacekeeping. It also revealed the complexity of decolonization when multiple outside powers had interests in its outcome. For these reasons, and others, the Congo intervention would be the last large peacekeeping operation during the remaining decades of the Cold War.

The United Nations returned to the Congo more than 40 years later. The second Congo crisis, also known as the Great Lakes crisis of 1997–2001, was the first large-scale African regional war of the postcolonial era. It attracted the forces of nine nation-states and at least 12 rebel factions, presenting the UN with a difficult set of challenges. Coming only a few years after crises in Somalia and Rwanda, the international community's timid response, and its almost total neglect of the conflict, underscored the widespread feeling of "humanitarian fatigue" that plagued the debates over sub-Saharan Africa in the 1990s.

The end of the Cold War removed the West's remaining rationales for supporting Mobutu's regime, who was subsequently overthrown in 1997 by a coalition of neighboring states utilizing forces led by the former Lumumba ally, Laurent Kabila, who proceeded to follow Mobutu's —and, reaching further back, Leopold's—model of extraction and exploitation. But several of the neighboring states who had aided in "liberating" the Congolese from the grip of Mobutu had their own designs on the resource-rich region. After falling out with Kabila, they launched a coordinated attack on the Congo. In April 1999 the Security Council harshly condemned those neighboring states with forces on Congolese territory and dispatched a special envoy to the region. A subsequent Security Council Resolution authorized the second United Nations intervention in the Congo in four decades. The Security Council called for a mere 5,000 peacekeepers but, considering the precedents, outside states remained reluctant to contribute forces and the UN had difficulty achieving desired force levels. The United Nations helped reach a negotiated truce, but Kabila's assassination in 2001, and the unsettled conditions surrounding the succession of his son, Joseph, led many to predict that the UN would need to return to the region.

More than four million people have died in the Congo's many civil conflicts, and this, one of the worst human tragedies of the post-Cold War era, receives scant mention in the West. Since the waning of the Cold War, the Congo is seen by many to have lost its strategic value.

Moreover, with nine national armies, a dozen rebel groups, and numerous local militias contending for the resource-rich region, the Congo crisis is considered too complicated, too intractable, and too distant, to comprehend.

The UN Challenges White Rule in Rhodesia, South Africa, Namibia. The persistence of white-dominated settlement colonies in southern Africa provoked a crisis over self-determination during the first four decades of the United Nations. White minority-ruled states such as Rhodesia and South Africa, and the South African-controlled territory of Namibia, seemed more and more anomalous in an Africa swept by the currents of independence, self-determination, and black majority rule.

Centuries of European colonization and settlement had profoundly changed the demographic patterns of southern Africa. The initial brutal defeat of the traditional indigenous chieftains was followed by white settlement and the importation of thousands of migrant laborers from Asia and other parts of Africa to establish massive extractive industries. Majority black populations in Rhodesia, South Africa, and Namibia found themselves exploited and were denied political, civil, economic, and human rights, as white minorities imposed institutionalized systems of segregation known by the Afrikaans word "apartheid."

The General Assembly grappled with the issue of white minority rule in southern Africa for more than four decades. The matter fell to the Assembly because the white-ruled regimes in southern Africa had powerful Western allies on the Security Council, such as Britain and the United States. They threatened to veto action, or even sanctions, against South Africa and did so more than 20 times. As elsewhere in Africa, self-determination in Rhodesia, South Africa, and Namibia became entangled in the Cold War. The Western powers backed white minority rule in southern Africa as a bastion of anticommunism in the region. They skirted sanctions, dispatched economic and military assistance to the white regimes, supported policies of coercion against the black population, and branded as terrorists those struggling against white oppression.

The British colony of Southern Rhodesia, established by Cecil Rhodes in the 1890s, had, since 1953, been part of a federation that included Northern Rhodesia and Nyasaland, where white settlers from all three components ruled over black majorities. After Northern Rhodesia and

Nyasaland achieved independence in 1964 as the black majority-ruled states of Zambia and Malawi, pressure increased on Southern Rhodesia to end white rule prior to its own independence. Instead, the white regime broke with Britain in 1965 and declared an independent state, modeled after the apartheid regime in neighboring South Africa. The United Nations took the innovative step of imposing economic sanctions on Rhodesia in 1966, the first time the UN had taken such action. Rhodesia, increasingly isolated and under the pressure of international sanctions, ultimately signed the Lancaster House Agreement of 1979, ending white rule.

In neighboring South Africa a bitter clash between British imperial aims in the region and Afrikaner, or Boer, nationalism, had given way to an equally violent struggle between blacks, who constituted the vast majority of the population, and whites, who comprised a small minority but ruled through the brutal system of apartheid. Few issues received more attention from the United Nations during its first five decades, and the urgency of its condemnations increased as the composition of the General Assembly changed owing to decolonization.

Apartheid, based upon racism and white supremacy, cruelly repressed the black population and employed state terrorism against supporters of black rights at home and their allies abroad. The apartheid regime linked racism and anticommunism as an ideology of state, and pursued a policy of regional destabilization by intervening in neighboring conflicts. The brutality of the apartheid system led the General Assembly to address the controversy during more than 200 debates since first addressing the question, at the request of India, in 1946. The South Africa controversy also laid bare the disagreements between the West and the developing world at the United Nations. Throughout the 1960s and 1970s a majority of the General Assembly fought to impose stricter sanctions against South Africa. That path was frequently blocked by the United States, Britain, and France who, concerned with South Africa's pivotal role in Cold War Africa, argued that sanctions violated South African sovereignty.

By the late 1980s, growing international opprobrium had made South Africa an isolated pariah state. In 1990 President F. W. de Klerk allowed the release of African National Congress leader Nelson Mandela, long proscribed as a terrorist in the West, after a quarter century of confinement. According to Karen Mingst and Margaret Karns, authors of *The United Nations in the Post-Cold War Era*, the United Nations played a large role in legitimizing the South African domestic opposition to apartheid. It also delegitimized the white regime, ultimately defeating apartheid. The UN's role in South Africa expanded in 1992, dispatching an observer mission to oversee the ongoing process of peace and reconciliation and to aid in the transition. These efforts led to the first open elections in South Africa in 1994, which resulted in a sweeping victory for Mandela and his party.

The crisis in neighboring Namibia was linked to the question of South Africa. In what some have seen as a genocidal prelude to the Holocaust, Germans began colonizing the region as German South West Africa in 1884. Their violent tactics reduced the local population, mostly Herero and Nama peoples, by an estimated 75 percent. The Germans promoted theories of racial superiority which rationalized the mass slaughter, and German administrators adopted the strategy of using concentration camps from the British imperial experience in neighboring South Africa. After World War I the region became a class "C" League of Nations mandate administered by South Africa which, after many decades of rule, introduced its repressive apartheid measures and sought to formally incorporate Namibia into its territory. The General Assembly responded by accusing South Africa of maladministration, calling for an end to South African rule, and declaring Namibia to be the direct responsibility of the UN. In 1971 the International Court of Justice declared South Africa's occupation of Namibia illegal. Namibia's future became hostage to the broader regional crisis during the Cold War, as South Africa provoked strife there and in neighboring Angola. After the shattering defeat of South African forces at Cuito Cuanavale (a victory for Cuban forces introduced to the region by Fidel Castro) in Angola in May 1988, Pretoria relented, opening the way for the establishment of the United Nations Transitional Assistance Group (UNTAG) in Namibia.

UNTAG became an early example of the new era—or "second generation"—of peacekeeping operations, its mission expanding well beyond traditional peacekeeping to monitoring the 1989 elections, aiding refugee populations, and repatriating 40,000 exiles. Having accomplished its mission, UNTAG departed Namibia in March 1990. Its achievement, Stanley Meisler has argued in *The United Nations: The First Fifty Years*, was an important contributing factor to the end of apartheid and the eventual introduction of election monitors to neighboring South Africa in 1994.

The United Nations and the Consequences of the Cold War in Africa. Independence came late to the former Portuguese colonies of Angola and Mozambique, and immediately became entangled in the geopolitical struggles of the Cold War. In Portuguese Africa the crisis of decolonization became inseparable from the Cold War as nowhere else, spawning civil wars in both nations with profound humanitarian consequences and challenging the United Nations on numerous levels.

Angola's experience of European contact and colonialism set the stage for its postcolonial crisis. Europeans subjected Angola to one of the most violent and disruptive slave experiences, the sociological consequences of which are still felt today. Even by the standards of Africa, the Portuguese colonial experience was particularly harsh and backward, so much so that Portugal refused to report to the UN on the status of its colonies. Portugal left a colony in economic and political chaos when independence was achieved in 1975, precipitating a civil war that became entangled in the ideological aims of the superpowers. According to William Minter, the divisions of tribal society in Angola were intensified by the politics of the Cold War, with the three largest tribal groups allying with various factions backed by either the Soviet Union, Cuba, South Africa, or the United States. The United Nations mounted four missions to Angola in the 1990s to verify the departure of foreign troops, monitor the implementation of peace accords, and promote reconciliation. But by 1999, with the UN's work only partly accomplished, Angola asked the UN to depart, leaving behind only a rudimentary UN presence to deal with the various combatants. Angola remains one of the most tragic legacies of Cold War Africa.

In Mozambique, civil war erupted a few years after independence, when a postcolonial Marxist government faced a growing resistance movement backed by the white regimes in neighboring Rhodesia and South Africa. The war raged for more than a decade but, by 1992, some progress toward peace had been achieved. The Security Council had authorized the deployment of more than 7,000 military and civilian personnel in an effort to implement a peace agreement, monitor a cease-fire among the factions, oversee the withdrawal of all foreign forces, and establish and observe the fragile electoral process.

Failure in Somalia and Rwanda. The crisis in Somalia engaged the United Nations like nothing before. The UN confronted the challenges of providing humanitarian relief on a massive scale, compounded by the collapse of the state institutions. The UN found itself overwhelmed by the anarchic conditions in Somalia. At least 15 armed factions vied for power. Coordinating a multinational peacekeeping force of nearly 40,000 troops from more than 20 nations, created the largest and most expensive UN operation to date. That the United States pursued different priorities and aims once in Somalia further complicated the UN's mission.

As Paolo Tipodi has shown in *The Colonial Legacy in Somalia*, the modern Somali state is a product of European imperialism. The Somali-speaking peoples are one of the largest ethnic groups in Africa and are scattered throughout the northeast of the continent. Precolonial Somalia was not a unified entity but a cluster of clan and kinship groups who subsisted by raising livestock. In the late nineteenth-century scramble for Africa, the British carved out a northern Somaliland protectorate, altering the centuries-old pastoral rhythms of life on the Horn of Africa. The French subsequently established French Somaliland (later to become Djibouti), and the Italians ultimately claimed southern Somalia in 1905. The Europeans further complicated the situation when they ceded the Ogaden region of historic Somalia to neighboring Ethiopia and a portion of southern Somalia to British Kenya.

The effort to create a modern nation-state proved disruptive to traditional society, where most Somalis looked to their clans for political identity, not a centralized state. After 1960 the British and Italian Somali colonies merged into an independent Somalia. The postcolonial state became entangled in the politics of the Cold War, as both Washington and Moscow sought control of the region owing to its strategic location on the Horn. The superpowers contributed to make Somalia's army the largest in Africa. When the Cold War regime of Said Barre was overthrown in 1991, Somalia descended into chaos. Clan identities and loyalties remained more important than loyalty to the new state, contributing to the fractured nature of Somali society. At the time of the UN intervention in 1992, the civil war and the subsequent famine had already taken an estimated 300,000 lives and another 4.5 million Somalis faced starvation.

The United Nations Operations in Somalia (UNOSOM) aimed to aid in the distribution of humanitarian relief and establish a secure environment for the delivery of further aid. But the chaotic conditions made the UN's humanitarian efforts difficult and, with US encouragement, the UN's mission in Somalia began to focus on political and security problems as the root of the humanitarian crisis. The UN forces, and particularly the US troops within them, became obsessed with political matters such as regime change, seeking to capture the clan leader Mohammed Farah Aidid. Subsequent efforts to disarm or capture Aidid resulted in the deaths of 24 Pakistani peacekeepers in the autumn of 1993. This was followed by bloody street-to-street fighting in downtown Mogadishu, which left 18 US peacekeepers dead. Faced by an angry and antagonized Somali population, plus sensational media coverage in the United States, President Clinton announced the withdrawal of US forces, crippling the UN's larger mission there.

The Somalia operation had enormous consequences. While the UN achieved some progress on the humanitarian front, the loss of 147 peacekeepers received most of the attention and had debilitating aftereffects, which led to a reassessment of peacekeeping and particularly nation building. Among other unhappy consequences, the United Nations made little progress establishing even the most basic of Somali state institutions. This provoked a debate over the UN's role in nation building beyond rudimentary peacekeeping. Somalia also undermined US support for UN operations, as the American public, fed a steady diet of media coverage critical of the operation, quickly grew impatient at the use of US forces in areas not vital to American interests. Somalia delivered a blow to those who had advocated that the United Nations should take an interest in humanitarian interventions. (*See Document No. 23.*) In his book *Clinton's World: Remaking American Foreign Policy,* William Hyland argues that while the humanitarian intervention in Somalia achieved much, saving thousands of lives, the Clinton administration planted the seeds of the UN's failure by expanding the mission and taking sides, chasing warlords, and rebuilding the failed Somali state along lines favored by Washington.

The debacle in Somalia had repercussions beyond the Horn of Africa. In Rwanda, the very recent memory of Somalia contributed to paralysis and the phenomenon of "humanitarian fatigue," which relegated the UN to the role of bystander, paralyzed, as 800,000 Rwandans were slaughtered in one of the worst acts of genocide since World War II.

The inhabitants of Rwanda—roughly 85 percent Hutu, 14 percent Tutsi, and 1 percent Twa—had loosely held their ethnic identities during the precolonial era. The colonial period began in 1899 with the arrival of the Germans, who polarized the distinctions among Rwandans, rigidifying the precolonial social order into a caste system. According to one of the premier observers of Rwanda's ethnography, Mahmood Mamdani, "The Germans understood Africa through the optic of late-nineteenth-century imperial Europe, which saw humanity as a conglomeration of races that required identification and hierarchical classification." The flexible identities of the precolonial period were frozen into a more rigid caste-like structure, and these distinctions were polarized by the colonial state. The racial identification and hierarchical ethnic classification continued after Germany relinquished the colony to Belgium as a League of Nations mandate in 1920. Belgium ruled Rwanda harshly, instituting ethnic politics that initially favored the minority Tutsi. The Belgians organized embryonic state institutions based on dubious racial theories, mandated ethnic pass cards, and expanded the advantages of the Tutsi elite. This eventually led to a mass exodus of a terrorized Hutu population into neighboring Uganda. After a Hutu uprising ended generations of Tutsi dominance in 1961, the Belgians departed. But Hutu ethnic pogroms had established a pattern, and subsequent frustrations over Rwanda's lack of economic development aggravated ethnic tensions.

These ethnic tensions reached a critical point following the assassination of Rwandan president Juvenal Habyarimana in April 1994. The massacre of Rwandan Prime Minister Agathe Uwilingiyimana, along with her contingent of Belgian bodyguards, provoked the evacuation of most foreign personnel in Rwanda. Those Rwandans who had sought refuge with the international community were abandoned, with the result that tens of thousands of Tutsies were massacred in international schools, churches, and hospitals. The international community responded with pious declarations of its good intentions, but little more. The commander of the previously established UN Assistance Mission in Rwanda (UNAMIR) repeatedly called for international support, but the United States, fearful of another Somalia, blocked any action. The Security Council avoided the use of the word "genocide" which, under the provisions of the Genocide Treaty, might have automatically committed the Security Council to take action.

In an unprecedented move, the Secretary General established an independent inquiry to investigate why the UN remained paralyzed while the Rwandan genocide unfolded. The inquiry concluded that a lack of will, compounded by diminished resources and ignorance about the ferocity of the violence, resulted in the UN's passive response. (*See Docu-*

ment No. 24.) The flood of Rwandan refugees into the area around Goma, Zaire, ignited the 1997 crisis in that neighboring country, resulting in the accession to power of Laurent Kabila in the Congo. Rwanda subsequently has been a major participant in the ghastly Great Lakes crisis that has claimed the lives of millions of Africans.

"Second Generation" Peacekeeping and Humanitarian Efforts in Africa.

The 1990s witnessed an explosion of United Nations activity throughout Africa, including peacekeeping, humanitarian relief, and conflict prevention. The UN's seventh Secretary General, Kofi Annan of Ghana, has sought to focus the world's attention on poverty, the HIV/AIDS crisis, and child combatants in Africa. As the former head of UN peacekeeping, and the first Secretary General from sub-Saharan Africa, he has articulated an "Annan Doctrine" positing that states cannot commit atrocities while hiding behind a veil of "sovereignty," and outside powers should reconsider humanitarian intervention in Africa.

The UN has become more active in all regions of Africa in the last decade. In the west African state of Liberia, a United Nations observer mission has, for the first time, worked with a regional peacekeeping operation already deployed by the Economic Organization of West African States (ECOWAS). Unlike much of the rest of Africa, Liberia's problems did not stem from traditional colonialism. They arose from less obvious neocolonial maladies such as uneven economic development, overdependence on raw materials, and difficulty in maintaining state institutions in a region organized along tribal lines of authority. The more immediate origins of the Liberian crisis of the 1990s lay in the IMF's suspension of aid in 1986, which precipitated widespread economic chaos and civil war and the near complete meltdown of state institutions and civil authority. Chaos in Liberia in the 1990s resulted in an estimated 150,000 deaths, nearly a million refugees, and the eventual displacement of nearly half the population. In 1993 the UN dispatched a peacekeeping observer mission to assist with the demobilization of combatants, facilitate deliveries of humanitarian aid, investigate human rights abuses, and monitor and verify elections.

Until 1961, neighboring Sierra Leone had been a British colony, created by forcing together 18 various ethnic groups and placing them within arbitrary and artificial borders. The UN responded to an ongoing civil war in the mid-1990s, leading to the deployment of an observer mission, again in cooperation with ECOWAS, seeking to restore order, monitor a cease-fire, and provide relief to hundreds of thousands of refugees and displaced persons.

The UN's longest peacekeeping operation in Africa remains its mission in the former Spanish colony of Western Sahara, where indigenous Saharawis, now largely based in Algeria, have struggled against Moroccan forces since 1976. The situation in Western Sahara had long been complicated by Cuban, Libyan, and Algerian backing for the Saharawi independence forces and US support for Morocco. After a UN-brokered cease-fire in 1991 the UN has sought, so far in vain, to hold a referendum to determine the region's ultimate status. The controversy has once again been complicated by Morocco's recent granting of long-term leases for oil exploration off the Western Saharan coast to French and American oil companies, which consequently have a keen interest in its ultimate disposition.

Less than a decade after the debacle in Somalia, the UN has again committed itself to peacekeeping in the Horn of Africa. In the summer of 2000, the UN established a peacekeeping operation to monitor the cessation of hostilities between Ethiopia and Eritrea. Numerous UN agencies also sought to relieve the regional humanitarian crisis that has been intensified by a drought and famine precipitated by the conflict.

The African continent, and particularly the sub-Saharan region, continues to confront the United Nations with an almost imponderable number of challenges in the areas of humanitarian relief, health care, peacekeeping, peacemaking, and economic development. Since the accession of Secretary General Annan, there has been renewed interest at the UN in the plight of the continent's most vulnerable. However, the West appears to have little desire to become more engaged in African problems. Now, more than four decades since the heady era of African decolonization, the annual United Nations Human Development Index, measuring life expectancy, educational attainment, and income levels, persistently places 25 African nations at the very bottom of its rankings. Among them are areas of substantial UN involvement such as the Congo, Sierra Leone, Rwanda, Angola, and Mozambique. (*See Document No. 25.*) Despite the UN's efforts in these and other regional matters, and despite the widening reach of UN operations and programs, sub-Saharan Africa remains the most neglected, underdeveloped, vulnerable part of the world.

CHAPTER 6

THE UNITED NATIONS AFTER
THE COLD WAR

New Possibilities for Change and Reform. The end of the Cold War fundamentally changed international politics and also offered the possibility of a new role for the United Nations in world affairs. The Cold War had cast a shadow over the UN throughout its first four decades. With the end of the East-West struggle, the paralysis that had plagued the Security Council seemingly disappeared overnight, inspiring much optimism for the UN to play a greater role in a new, post-Cold War, world order. This initial optimism was not completely warranted. The United Nations would have new opportunities, but also faced a host of new challenges, as the end of the Cold War ignited unanticipated crises, new demands, and a reprioritization of the UN's mission. There would be renewed calls for reform of the UN's institutions and its methods of conducting business. It would also confront the challenge of resurgent nationalism, separatism, and ethnic conflict. These would demand innovative responses, particularly in the area of conflict prevention, peacekeeping, and nation building. The East-West conflict had receded, but North-South tensions over trade and economic development continued as before and, in some ways, have been intensified by globalization and the breakdown of the Cold War international order. The end of the Cold War introduced new regions of UN concern, including parts of the world where the UN had been largely excluded previously, such as the Balkans, Central America, the Caribbean, and the former Soviet republics. New challenges erupted as globalization and, after 2001, an increasing trend in the United States in favor of unilateralism, intervention, and preemption would once again threaten to marginalize the United Nations.

Developments such as the collapse of the Soviet empire, and revolutions in Russia, Central Europe, and much of Latin America, ushered in a new era in relations among states. But the window of opportunity to create a truly new world order with a reinvigorated United Nations at its center arrived and subsequently passed. An important opportunity was largely lost. The dissolution of the USSR left no power but the

United States to lead the way, and Washington met the challenge with remarkable shortsightedness.

The question of reform topped the agenda of the United Nations after the Cold War, but reform has always been a matter of perspective, as members demanded vastly different changes. Member states traditionally favor reforms that will promote their interests within the UN. The developing world often advocates reform of the UN's associated trade and financial institutions, such as the IMF and World Bank, and pushes for reforming how GATT and the WTO do business. But it also favors structural reforms that might play to their advantage, such as enhancement of the role of the General Assembly and changes on the Security Council.

To many, the Security Council is an anachronism dominated by the nominal allies of World War II. Large powers such as Japan, the European Union, India, Brazil, even Nigeria, have emphasized reform, or expansion, of the composition of the permanent members of the Security Council and reconsideration of their veto power. The end of the Cold War restored some sanity to the use of the Security Council veto. In the aftermath of the 1991 Gulf War there were no vetoes cast in the next two sessions. The United States has used the veto on ten occasions since the end of the Cold War, Russia three times, China twice. (*See Document No. 26.*)

The United States has at times sought to diminish the role of the General Assembly, which it has often perceived as a mere debating society hostile to US interests. As the largest contributor to the UN (*See Document No. 27.*) Washington has also demanded numerous cost-saving measures. Yet this occurred at the exact time that the US also demanded more of the UN's limited resources by calling for the United Nations to take on more responsibilities, particularly in the areas of peacekeeping, humanitarian relief, and nation building. Reform of any sort is difficult because the UN Charter is very difficult to amend. Amendments require a two-thirds majority of the General Assembly, as well as all five of the permanent members of the Security Council. While many worthy reforms are debated, the prospect of achieving them remains daunting.

With the end of the Cold War, the United States has become the world's preeminent military and economic power. Washington has grown increasingly impatient with building international consensus to support its global aims. US policy has often been chauvinistic regarding the

UN, as many Americans believe Washington should pursue its interests without the need to cooperate with anyone, particularly the UN. Although many public opinion polls continue to demonstrate support for the United Nations, the United States began withholding a percentage of its dues (following the precedent established by the Soviet Union during the Congo crisis) to pressure the UN in the mid-1980s. Washington has removed UN officials it has deemed inimical to US interests, such as its refusal to support Boutros Boutros-Ghali for a second term as Secretary General, and orchestrating the removal of two UN High Commissioners for Human Rights, Theo van Boven and, more recently, Mary Robinson, one of the most senior women in the history of the United Nations.

Robinson's fate, however, obscures an often overlooked aspect of change at the United Nations: the growing influence of women in all levels of its institutions. While the increasing trend in favor of personnel from the global South has been well examined, the expanding role of women at the UN has also changed the tenor of the Secretariat and other UN-related institutions. Women have played important roles in the United Nations, from Anne O'Hare McCormick's contributions to postwar planning to Eleanor Roosevelt's role in drafting the Universal Declaration of Human Rights, but it was only after the UN's Decade for Women (1975–1985) that significant progress became obvious. There has yet to be a woman Secretary General, but women have now occupied all other major positions in the United Nations, from heading peacekeeping operations, to leading major commissions such as refugees and human rights, to prominent roles on the International Court of Justice and war crimes tribunals.

Redefining Peacekeeping and Nation Building. Since the end of the Cold War, peacekeeping has emerged as one of the most visible, and the most contentious, endeavors of the United Nations. While peacekeeping is not mentioned in the UN Charter, it has been an evolving concept, born of necessity and implemented on an ad hoc basis. Scholars of peacekeeping divide its history into two segments: a "first generation" featuring more narrowly defined missions, beginning with a modest effort to monitor the border between Greece and Bulgaria in 1947 and two subsequent observer missions in the Middle East and Kashmir; and a much more expansive "second generation" in the years after the Cold War, beginning with the 1989 effort in Namibia to provide humanitarian relief, repatriate refugees, educate voters, and oversee elections.

Although the earliest examples of peacekeeping were monitoring or observer missions, the "first generation" also included three larger missions featuring armed multinational forces: the dispatch of up to 6,000 troops in response to the 1956 Suez Crisis; the deployment of 20,000 troops in the Congo after 1960; and the smaller, but more enduring, effort in Cyprus after 1964. The politics of the Cold War narrowed the options for peacekeeping, with Moscow becoming increasingly hostile to such undertakings after the controversial experiment in the Congo. The subsequent Cyprus peacekeeping mission occurred, in part, because there were so few obvious Cold War issues at stake. During more than four decades of the Cold War, the UN launched only 13 peacekeeping operations.

Following Mikhail Gorbachev's December 1988 address before the General Assembly, when he called for the United Nations to take the lead in establishing a new order in international politics, peacekeeping evolved in new and controversial directions. This "second generation" of peacekeeping was notable for the growing degree of consensus among the permanent five members of the Security Council—particularly Washington and Moscow—over the aims of peacekeeping. There was also an increasing, although not exclusive, focus on intrastate conflicts, as opposed to conflicts between states. It's role in peacekeeping, peacemaking, and nation building also expanded. (*See Document No. 28.*)

The new era of cooperation among the permanent five also signaled a willingness to allow the United Nations to play a role in areas of primary interest to the superpowers previously considered off limits. For example, although unthinkable only a few years before, Moscow raised relatively few objections to UN involvement in the several crises in the former Yugoslavia in the 1990s, or to a UN role in former Soviet republics such as Georgia and Tajikistan. Starting in 1989, Washington also allowed the UN a role in its own Cold War sphere of influence in Central America and the Caribbean, where the United Nations launched observer missions and moderate nation-building efforts first in Nicaragua, and later, in El Salvador, Haiti, and Guatemala.

In Asia the UN embarked upon a huge peacekeeping operation in Cambodia, comprising 20,000 UN personnel from more than 100 nations, supported by all the permanent members of the Security Council, including the United States and its erstwhile rival, the People's Republic of China. UN peacekeepers took on unprecedented responsibilities in developing and administering various aspects of the state. It oversaw the implementation of a comprehensive settlement seeking to end a quarter century of conflict rooted in the Vietnam War era, which had already resulted in the deaths of an estimated two million Cambodians. As discussed previously in Chapter 5, post-Cold War peacekeeping operations have become most active in Africa, achieving much in places such as Namibia and, to a lesser extent, Mozambique. But it also suffered several well-publicized failures, most notably in Somalia, which had a profound impact on thinking about the capabilities of UN peacekeeping operations. These failures helped mute the response to both the Rwandan genocide and the subsequent Great Lakes Crisis. UN peacekeeping has nonetheless expanded into areas such as Liberia, Sierra Leone, Western Sahara, and the dispute between Ethiopia and Eritrea.

The initial era of decolonization has passed, but the consequences of the colonial period and its aftermath continue to challenge the institutions of the United Nations. At the dawn of a new century, peacekeeping, for all of the controversy surrounding it, appears to have revitalized the original vision of Franklin Roosevelt and his postwar planners. They envisioned an elaborate system of international trusteeship in which the UN would assist in the process of decolonization. Their concept of trusteeship anticipated recent experiments in "second generation" peacekeeping and nation building, as it sought to smooth the process of self-determination by aiding in conflict resolution and nation building long before those concepts became commonplace in international discourse. As Roosevelt and several of his planners envisioned, a system of international trusteeship, rooted in an institution such as the United Nations, would possess a legitimacy, and even moral stature, that would be absent in efforts by sovereign great powers with their imperial pasts. Only an international organization could pursue nation building without the almost inevitable tendency of outside powers seeking selfish advantage. The Cold War struggle blocked Roosevelt's vision for almost half a century, but today, with the potential for cooperation among the permanent five, multilateral approaches to peacekeeping and nation building are more likely. However, a number of potentially destabilizing global hot spots persist where UN peacekeepers have been excluded and, in all likelihood, will continue to be excluded, such as the Israeli-occupied territories and Indian-occupied Kashmir.

For a time, Roosevelt also embraced the notion that the United Nations should include a number of associated regional bodies that would manage decolonization and nation building in their respective areas of responsibility. The regional concept ultimately disappeared from the administration's postwar plans, but recent collaborative peacekeeping endeavors between the United Nations and the Organization of American States, the Organization for Security and Cooperation in Europe, NATO, the Organization of African Unity, and the Economic Organization of West African States, have demonstrated the potential of regional approaches to peacekeeping and nation building.

The UN Confronts Multiple Crises in the Former Yugoslavia. In the former Yugoslavia, United Nations peacekeeping faced unprecedented challenges during a violent conflict among well-armed combatants who were often supported by neighboring states. Efforts at establishing an arms embargo and so-called UN safe areas, and the UN role in numerous efforts at peacemaking—particularly in Bosnia—proved controversial and, ultimately, unsuccessful. Other innovations, such as the preventive force sent to Macedonia and the state-building efforts launched in Kosovo, met with varying degrees of progress, although in both cases the underlying problems are far from resolved.

At the end of the First World War the international community aided in the creation of the Kingdom of the Serbs, Croats, and Slovenes—which ultimately became Yugoslavia, the land of the south Slavs. It seemed natural that the disintegration of the Yugoslav state in the 1990s would once again involve the international community. For the United Nations, the breakup of the former Yugoslavia is a story of bitter lessons learned though traumatic experiences, and serves as one of the most controversial chapters in the post-Cold War United Nations.

United Nations involvement in the breakup of Yugoslavia began in September 1991—with the imposition of an arms embargo on the region —and quickly expanded, starting in Croatia, which declared its independence in June 1991. The Security Council established the United Nations Protection Force (UNPROFOR) to establish safe areas in Croatia. It also sought to stabilize the crisis and worked to bring a truce. UNPROFOR faced enormous difficulties, its mandate constantly expanding as it faced new crises.

Neighboring Bosnia-Herzegovina, a nation of 3.7 million people with a diverse ethnic distribution (estimated in 1990 at 44 percent Bosnian Muslim, 31 percent Serb, and 17 percent Croat), became the scene of the worst European war crimes since World War II. The United Nations deployed another peacekeeping force (UNPROFOR II), banned the overflight of Serbian planes, and ultimately declared six Bosnian cities —Srebrenica, Sarajevo, Gorazda, Zepa, Tuzla, Bihac—United Nations-protected "safe areas." Peacekeepers soon discovered that they could not protect their established safe havens. Several fell to Serb militias, with especially gruesome consequences in the eastern Bosnian town of Srebrenica, where an estimated 7,000 Bosnian Muslims, gathered in the town seeking UN protection, were systematically slaughtered with UN forces billeted nearby. UNPROFOR II also was unable to lift the protracted sieges of Sarajevo and Mostar, despite periodic deliveries of humanitarian aid. Ultimately, more than 200,000 Bosnians, many of them Muslim civilians, were killed, and many more became refugees. The Bosnian debacle remains one of the most profound and tragic legacies of the post–Cold War United Nations. (*See Document No. 29.*)

In Macedonia, a potentially explosive political situation has so far been largely forestalled owing to the adroit maneuverings of the international community. At the height of the turmoil, the UN grew increasingly alarmed at the possibility of Serbian intervention in Macedonia, a nation of slightly more than 1.5 million people. Equally alarming was the prospect of conflict between the state's estimated 900,000 Slav Macedonians and 600,000 ethnic Albanians, or a war between Macedonia and neighboring Albania. Another peacekeeping force was dispatched to Macedonia (UNPROFOR III), and, later, a United Nations Preventive Deployment Force (UNPREDEP) arrived to monitor Macedonia's borders with both Yugoslavia and Albania and aid in the distribution of humanitarian relief. UNPROFOR III and UNPREDEP became the first ever United Nations peacekeeping forces to have preventive mandates, and their mission in Macedonia continued for several years. "The deterrent here lay in the fact that the Security Council demonstrated its interest in the situation," notes Gareth Evans, one of the leading observers of preventive peacekeeping, "all the relevant parties were under close international scrutiny, and there was at least an implication of willingness to take further action if there were any resort to violence."

The United Nations also played an expansive role in the semiautonomous Yugoslav province of Kosovo, which was dragged into the regional crisis by Yugoslav president Slobodan Milosevic's effort to crush the ethnic Albanian desire to form an independent state. The Serb invasion produced an estimated 1 million refugees and prompted NATO's first ever military action, directed against Serb positions in both Kosovo and neighboring Serbia. In the aftermath of the NATO bombing campaign, the Security Council deployed the United Nations Interim Administration for Kosovo (UNMIK) in June 1999, which sought to restore civil order and establish interim state institutions. The United Nations continues to support Kosovo's autonomy, nominally as part of the Federal Republic of Yugoslavia, but the future of Kosovo as part of a larger Serbia is increasingly doubtful, given recent events, leaving its ultimate status uncertain.

Assessments of the UN's multifaceted and complex role in the former Yugoslavia remain controversial. Debate rages over whether most of the blame for the flawed response to the crisis should lie with (1) the United Nations itself, and particularly its peacekeeping operations in the region; or (2) the members of the Security Council, which consistently saddled the United Nations with new responsibilities and mandates but lacked the will to provide it with sufficient resources to carry them out; or (3) with specific European nations that remained paralyzed in the face of mounting human rights violations and war crimes. Whatever the case, the wars of the former Yugoslavia, particularly its Bosnian theater, revealed the inability of the United Nations, once engaged, to end the conflict. Most serious was its failure to protect its own safe havens. In Bosnia, the UN's failures ultimately led to its gradual replacement by other organizations, such as the Organization for Security and Cooperation in Europe (OSCE) and NATO, particularly in the areas of peace enforcement, peacemaking, and nation building. The UN experience there—along with the simultaneous Somalia debacle—contributed toward cooling the optimism about the role of the United Nations in world affairs after the paralysis of the Cold War.

The Balkans have been supplanted in the headlines, but the UN continues to play a significant role there, including in the international trial at the Hague of Milosevic, and the convictions of senior figures from the Balkan crisis of the 1990s, including Biljana Plavsic, former president of the Serb Republic of Bosnia-Herzegovina. Yugoslavia's disintegration has thus far created five new members of the General Assembly: Slovenia, Croatia, Bosnia-Herzegovina, Macedonia, and a rump Serbian Republic. The long-term status of Montenegro, and particularly Kosovo, is yet to be determined.

New Opportunities for the UN in Post-Cold War Central America and the Caribbean. The end of the Cold War opened possibilities for UN intervention in the Balkans and former Soviet republics such as Georgia and Tajikistan. At the same time, the UN also moved into areas of the Western Hemisphere once largely off limits owing to US domination of the region. The United States had long seen Central America and the Caribbean as its exclusive sphere of interest. In keeping with Cold War practices it supported client states in the region and sought to undermine or overthrow uncooperative governments. But the many repressive regimes failed to address the acute social, economic, and political problems of their societies, often legacies of the socioeconomic disparities of the colonial era. The chief regional body, the Organization of American States (OAS), had often been discredited by its frequent support for the Cold War containment doctrine in the region and its involvement in the intervention in Guatemala in 1954 to overthrow President Jacobo Arbenz, its expulsion of Castro's Cuba in 1962, and its intervention in the Dominican Republic in 1965. Because the United Nations had little previous record of involvement in the Hemisphere during the Cold War, its operations in the region had a high degree of legitimacy.

A United Nations Observer Group in Central America (ONUCA), launched in 1989 with US consent, monitored the 1990 Nicaraguan elections which resulted in the defeat of the Sandinista regime. The UN subsequently worked alongside the OAS, facilitating the transition to peacemaking and reaching an agreement to demobilize the US-backed Contra rebels. In El Salvador, a tiny Central American nation with a long history of civil conflict, and beset by a ghastly civil war for more than a decade, the United Nations introduced an observer mission in 1991 to monitor a cease-fire and implement a peace agreement. In what Stanley Meisler calls the most remarkable achievement of the UN during the tenure of Secretary General Perez de Cuellar, UN peacekeepers oversaw the reduction of armed forces in the country, the creation of a new police force, the reform of the judicial and electoral systems, the enforcement of human rights, and nascent efforts at land reform. In neighboring Guatemala, United Nations peacekeepers performed similar duties in seeking to end a violent conflict that had raged since the overthrow of President Arbenz in 1954.

The Caribbean nation of Haiti, formerly a colony of France, has long been the poorest in the Western Hemisphere. Its history of poverty and a shocking maldistribution of wealth contributed to its instability, repressive governments, human rights violations, and lack of democracy. As the Cold War wound down, the United Nations oversaw the election of Jean-Bertrand Aristide, a Catholic priest supported by many of Haiti's poor. But Aristide's reforms quickly ran afoul of the Haitian military and ruling elite, and he was overthrown in a military coup in September 1991. The United Nations cooperated with the OAS and the United States to have Aristide restored to power, and all three cooperated in building infrastructure and reforming the Haitian military and other state institutions. Amidst much controversy, Aristide was once again driven from power and into exile in early 2004.

The Global Environment, World Health, Human Rights. The post–Cold War era inspired a renewed focus at the United Nations on the issues of the global environment, world health, and human rights. Prior to 1972 there had been little attention to environmental questions at the United Nations, but a World Conference on the Human Environment was convened in Stockholm that year. Increasingly, an effort is being made to approach international environmental questions in a coordinated, global, way. The challenges are many, as individual nation-states frequently resent global cooperative approaches to environmental problems and see any effort to do so as an infringement on their sovereignty. Yet the United Nations currently remains the only available forum to launch a multinational effort to create some semblance of international standards for using the world's natural resources and for protecting the global environment. The Rio and Kyoto meetings on the status of the international environment are examples of this effort.

Much of the UN effort on global health has been channeled through the World Health Organization (WHO), which came into existence in 1948. One of the WHO's shining moments occurred in 1980 when it announced eradication of the deadly smallpox virus. The United Nations has also struggled with mobilizing various efforts to respond to the HIV/AIDS pandemic. The UN estimates that more than 15,000 people are infected with HIV/AIDS every day, and as many as 40 million have HIV/AIDS. Of these, 75 percent are in Africa, where AIDS is now the leading cause of death. As most national governments, particularly in the developing world, are overwhelmed by the crisis, the UN can play a role.

A number of World Health Organization efforts have stirred controversy, such as its recommendation that all governments provide medical insurance to all citizens. Proposed family planning efforts continue to provoke opposition in parts of the Third World, as well as within the United States. United Nations efforts to promote family planning have often run into a firestorm of controversy and opposition over abortion and even less invasive forms of family planning. In the face of much opposition, the United Nations Population Fund (UNFPA) has sought to provide families, and especially women, with education about family planning. According to UN figures, in the 1960s only 10 percent of the world's families practiced any method of family planning. The number now stands at more than 50 percent, with the result that women in developing countries are having far fewer children, from six births per woman in the 1960s to 3.5 by 2000.

Human rights are mentioned seven times in the United Nations Charter, and the promotion of human rights remains a cornerstone of the organization. In reaction to the violence and genocide of World War II, the international community produced the Universal Declaration on Human Rights in December 1948. (*See Document No. 30.*) The Declaration has been adopted by all nations of the world and the international community has declared the universality of the rights of all peoples. Its actual application has been much more problematic. Controversies have arisen over the degree to which the United Nations could seek to enforce universal standards of human rights in a world of diverse, sovereign states. Furthermore, different states have radically different notions of what constitutes human rights. Emotional disputes over such questions continue to divide the United Nations. Former Irish President Mary Robinson, the United Nations High Commissioner for human rights, was forced to step down from that position on September 11, 2002, in part because of her questioning of the human rights records of various states and her criticism of the US war on terrorism.

The United Nations and International Terrorism. The United Nations was created as a response to terrorism, the terrorism of a "total" world war that deliberately targeted civilian populations and took the lives of tens of millions. Human extermination occurred on a massive scale during World War II. To the staggering human losses of the Holocaust, the horrific deliberate assaults on civilian populations on the Eastern Front, the Japanese war on China, are added the names of terroristic infamy such as Guernica, Nanking, Rotterdam, Coventry, Dresden, Lidice, Tokyo, Leningrad, and Warsaw.

The United Nations did not discover the issue of terrorism recently; it has dealt with it over many years and was discussing the crisis in Afghanistan and its potential consequences in the months prior to the attacks of September 2001. Security Council Resolutions 1267 of October 15, 1999 and 1333 of December 19, 2000 called for sanctions against the Taliban regime in Afghanistan, freezing of their assets, destruction of terrorist training camps, and the expulsion of Al-Qaeda leader Osama bin Laden from Afghanistan. (*See Document No. 31.*) The attacks on New York and Washington in September 2001 reinforced the UN's focus on terrorism. Within hours of the attacks, the Security Council passed Resolution 1368, an unequivocal condemnation of the attacks, followed by Resolution 1373, which obligated all member states, under Chapter VII of the UN Charter (*see Document No. 10*), to deny all forms of support or safe haven to terrorist groups. The UN also established a special Counter Terrorism Committee (CTC) to assist member states in carrying out Resolutions 1368 and 1373.

Despite such prompt and unambiguous action in the days after the attacks, the United Nations has struggled to organize collective responses at the international level to terrorist outrages, whether they are in the form of state terrorism, or terrorism by non-state actors. A precise definition has remained elusive. Most member nations have, at some time or another, supported Resolutions condemning terrorism, including the attacks of September 2001; but a major challenge for the UN in fashioning a uniform response to terrorism is that there is absolutely no agreement at the international level on what precisely constitutes terrorism. After all, most nations, whatever their own aims and tactics, justify the use of state violence in the service of the noblest of aims in defense of their peoples or homelands. Traditional nation-states, for example, argue that terrorism is largely the practice of shadowy non-state entities. Indeed, the terrorist acts of organizations such as Al-Qaeda, Abu Sayyaf, the Irish Republican Army, or the Basque ETA have grabbed most of the headlines. But some have argued at the UN that powerful nation states persist in carrying out attacks on civilian populations to achieve their aims in international politics, while insisting that only non-state actors are terroristic. Surely, it is argued, the indiscriminate killing of civilians by nation states is also a form of terrorism.

The events of September 2001 offered the prospect of closer cooperation between the US and UN on a number of issues, such as what to do about failed states, nation building, and the proliferation of nuclear weapons. But rather than bringing Washington and the United Nations together in the struggle against terrorism, the post-9/11 years drove a deeper wedge between them. The divergence arose over what constitutes terrorism, and because the United States sought to use the attacks to redefine its overseas interests and launch a new doctrine of preemptive or preventive war. Washington subsequently posited that a preemptive war against Iraq, for example, was linked to the war on terror. But the United States could not persuade skeptical allies and others in the Security Council to support this view. Many on the Council remained dubious that Iraq had a role in the attacks of 2001. They also doubted that the US possessed intelligence superior to that of UN weapons inspectors, or that Iraq was producing weapons of mass destruction and preparing to use them. The new doctrine of preemptive force alarmed many at the UN because it threatened to undermine the most basic principles of preventive diplomacy and collective security.

In the face of these challenges, Secretary General Annan sought to use the UN as a forum for examining terrorism in depth. His broader perspectives, such as the relationship between underdevelopment and support for terrorism and other "root causes," were unpopular and largely ignored in the US. "Terrorism is a weapon for alienated, desperate people, and often a product of despair," Annan said in 2002. "If human beings everywhere are given real hope of achieving self-respect and a decent life by peaceful methods, terrorists will become much harder to recruit, and will receive far less sympathy and support from society at large. Therefore, while we certainly need vigilance to prevent acts of terrorism, and firmness in condemning and punishing them, it will be self-defeating if we sacrifice other key priorities—such as human rights —in the process."

The Challenge of Globalization. While international terrorism has attracted the most attention at the beginning of the new century, the controversy over globalization remains one of the most complex challenges facing the United Nations. Some, such as Secretary General Annan, have argued that the chronic problems of the developing world and the sources of terrorism are linked and unaddressed economic grievances are contributing factors in fueling despair and extremism. Like terrorism, perspectives on globalization vary from state to state, region to region. Differences over how best to achieve global growth, and unaddressed problems brought about by globalization, have aggravated the North-South struggle. Taking the long view, these differences have the potential to become more destabilizing to the UN system than global terrorism.

The United Nations, and particularly institutions in the broader UN system such as the World Bank, the International Monetary Fund, and the World Trade Organization, are at the center of the many controversies over globalization. As Nobel Laureate Joseph Stiglitz has argued in *Globalization and Its Discontents,* critics of globalization charge that international economic institutions continue to serve the interests of the industrialized world. Increasingly, critics have confronted meetings of the WTO, IMF, and World Bank in places like Seattle, Cancun, Washington, Prague, and Melbourne. The views of these critics, however dimly understood in the West, reflect an increasingly vocal segment of global public opinion challenging the prevailing wisdom about international economics and development. These worldwide mass demonstrations seek to focus attention on issues such as Third World debt and reform of international economic institutions. The United States and Europe maintain that the proper foundation of international economic policy remains the Bretton Woods institutions and emphasize the pursuit of development through the "Washington Consensus" of increased trade, deregulation, and market liberalization. Developing nations argue that the rules of global trade have been tilted in favor of the major industrialized nations, causing the world's most economically vulnerable to fall deeper into debt and despair. In agriculture, for example, where the global South has some advantages, the IMF itself estimates that if the wealthy nations repealed their own trade barriers and farm subsidies the economic benefits to the South could be in excess of $100 billion per annum.

The UN faces the challenge of how to invigorate institutions of globalization in ways that can re-enfranchise the peoples of the world and instill confidence that international economic bodies are dedicated to improving lives in all parts of the world. Secretary General Annan's "Global Compact" initiative, originating from the 1999 Davos World Economic Forum, aims to encourage corporations to embrace a set of core principles through partnerships with UN agencies on matters of environmental protection, human rights, and labor standards. Critics fear that the Global Compact jeopardizes the UN's integrity, and allows corporations to use the UN's stamp of approval to pursue their own aims. Still, as Paul Taylor has noted in *International Organization in the Age of Globalization*, the UN is the only truly global institution with the legitimacy to spotlight and counterbalance the abuses and inequities of globalization.

The end of the Cold War had encouraged much optimism. It inspired hope that as the East-West confrontation declined, it would be replaced by mutually cooperative efforts to improve the living standards of nearly 5 billion people living below the international poverty threshold. Many hoped the end of the Cold War might inspire a new era of cooperation between North and South and a renewed focus on globalization and international development. "Ironically," Robert Gregg writes in *About Face: The United States and the United Nations*, "the end of the Cold War seems temporarily to have made attention to the problems of developing countries of the South by the industrialized countries of the North less, rather than more, likely." Now, more than a decade after the Cold War, the promise of globalization has remained just a promise. In some cases, globalization has contributed to the further maldistribution of the world's wealth. The one-fifth of the world's population that lives in the highest income areas accounts for more than 85 percent of the global Gross Domestic Product. The most current estimates are that even as the world's population grows from today's 6 billion to more than 9 billion by the year 2050, nearly 90 percent will still live in the most developmentally backward areas of the world.

CHAPTER 7

CONCLUSION: THE UNITED NATIONS IN THE TWENTY-FIRST CENTURY

An Alternative to Empire. The end of the Cold War opened new horizons for the United Nations and created expectations that it would emerge as the focus of world politics. But many events since then—particularly in Somalia, Rwanda, Bosnia, and Iraq—have shaken confidence in international institutions. A history of the UN's activities since the Cold War conjures up names of recent infamy, such as Sarajevo, Mogadishu, Kigali, and Srebrenica. These crises, with their images of failure and impotence in the face of violence, undermined much of the optimism that greeted the end of the Cold War.

The UN's shortcomings and debacles have been relatively easy to recount, as done herein. The achievements are complex and therefore more difficult to assess, in part because historians often lack effective methodologies for measuring acts of prevention. The challenge to historians and other social scientists, is finding ways of discussing what *didn't* happen. For example, how the United Nations often helped keep the Cold War from becoming a hot war. Just as important is how the UN has provided an alternative to empire in the post-1945 period. The UN worked to ease decolonization, first in Indonesia, then throughout much of Africa and the Middle East, where the UN contributed to halting an imperial war over Suez in 1956.

Most obviously, "World War Three" never occurred. One major achievement of the United Nations is in establishing norms of behavior, which may help to explain why, since 1945, we have been spared another war that could have upset the international system. During the Korean War the participation of the United Nations, and its moderating influence, may have prevented the fighting from enlarging into a conflict beyond the Korean Peninsula. The UN has also been given the mandate to deal with crises left by the Cold War in places like Angola, Mozambique, Cambodia, and the Congo. It has made considerable progress in El Salvador, Namibia, and East Timor. And while the UN's experience in Bosnia deservedly receives the most attention, UN preventive forces dispatched to nearby Macedonia may have averted another Bosnia.

An estimated 30 million people have perished in more than 150 armed conflicts during the first six decades of the United Nations. This would seem, on the face of it, a stinging indictment of the UN's efforts to prevent or resolve deadly violent conflict. However, in the three decades prior to the UN, an estimated 75 million died in armed conflicts, most particularly the cataclysmic world wars among the great powers. The post-1945 era has been relatively less violent, particularly if global population growth is considered. One distinctive feature of post-1945 conflicts, however, is that the majority of casualties in modern conflicts are likely to be civilians. Civilian casualties have provoked an international refugee crisis. The United Nations High Commissioner for Refugees estimates there are 20 million external refugees worldwide, and another 25 million displaced persons within their states of origin. The UN, with institutions already in place to respond to this problem, can continue to provide relief and repatriation, as well as spotlighting the plight of refugees.

The numerous crises at the beginning of the new millennium have renewed important questions about the effectiveness of the United Nations in meeting the challenges of the twenty-first century. The first six decades of the United Nations witnessed numerous successes and failures. The UN managed to avoid many of the problems that plagued the League of Nations, but it failed to emerge as the engine of a truly new world order. The UN has proven more effective than the League partly because it is much more representative. At its peak the League had only 58 members, as much of the world—particularly in Africa, Asia, and the Middle East—remained submerged under the control of European imperial power. Major powers such as the United States never joined, while Germany and the Soviet Union were initially kept out. Also, since the advent of the United Nations, none of the great powers have sought to truly overturn the international system in ways the revisionist powers of the 1930s such as Germany, Japan, and Italy sought to in the time of the League.

For all of its faults, the United Nations has also proved to be more adaptable than the League. While the UN Charter remains nearly impossible to amend, and substantial structural reforms would require the unlikely support of many nations that would be affected (several of them possessing a Security Council veto over such reform), the UN has demonstrated that it can change and evolve in informal ways. The evolution of peacekeeping, for example, or the more recent experiments with nation building, has revealed that the UN can respond to changes in the international system. Expansion of UN responsibilities in the area of humanitarian aid were also not originally envisioned by the UN's founders, yet it has made strides in working with, and through, regional organizations, many of which may have more structural flexibility in responding to crises.

The UN must continue to prove that it can be relevant in a changing world, and it must avoid being marginalized as it was during much of the Cold War, when both the Soviet Union and the United States excluded the United Nations from their areas of primary interest. This may prove easier than it seems, as it may become increasingly difficult for any power to project its power unilaterally. The permanent members of the Security Council have grown, for the most part, more interested in cooperation than confrontation, and they appear to have less interest in marginalizing the UN, as did the US and USSR during the Cold War.

The UN must remain adaptable to the challenges of a changing world order. It must find some means of addressing the widening gap in living standards between the global North and South and it needs to find a way to address the threats raised by globalization. Secretary General Kofi Annan's responses demonstrate that the UN understands some of the problems developing nations face in an age of rapid globalization. But the UN can achieve little without the leadership and cooperation of the great powers. The UN also needs to create an infrastructure to address the growing global environmental crisis. The wealthy nations have largely missed the opportunity to use the UN to address environmental problems from a multilateral perspective—probably the only way they can be addressed. They may soon recognize their shortsightedness as the global South continues to develop. The emergence of a large middle class in the developing world—now comprising hundreds of millions, soon billions, of people—with its concomitant consumer and resource demands, may force the developed West to recognize the narrowness of prevailing attitudes about the global environment.

As mentioned previously, the end of the Cold War opened numerous areas for UN involvement that were once considered the exclusive domain of the superpowers. Among them are Central America and the Caribbean, the Balkans, and former Soviet Republics such as Tajikistan and Georgia. A number of important flash points remain, such as the Israeli-Palestinian conflict and the India-Pakistan dispute, where the UN could play a greater role in promoting bilateral measures to avert further wars that threaten to involve various weapons of mass destruction, including nuclear weapons. The United Nations may also find that it has a larger role to play yet in the various crises in the Middle East. The UN has long been excluded from peacemaking efforts in the Israeli-Palestinian crisis, other than on humanitarian and refugee issues. Meanwhile, Middle East tensions have grown much worse, and some outside powers, such as the United States, have become increasingly compromised politically in the region. Furthermore, the violence of the ongoing Iraq war, and growing US occupation fatigue there, has raised the possibility of another long-term commitment for the United Nations.

In Africa, the United Nations will continue to play an active role, particularly in the sub-Saharan region, which has been removed from a Cold War framework but is still suffering the aftereffects of that struggle. Owing, in part, to the chaos stirred throughout Africa by the colonial powers, many humanitarian crises there will continue. Aside from UN efforts to stem famine and prevent the spread of the devastating HIV/AIDS plague, the UN will also play a role in adjudicating disputes and providing peacekeeping support. Sub-Saharan Africa remains one of the most neglected regions of an increasingly globalized world, and it will desperately need outside assistance in the decades ahead to prevent crises such as those that occurred in the 1990s in Rwanda and the Great Lakes region. The UN offers, at the very least, an opportunity to provide a global platform for drawing the attention of the international community to Africa's needs. Recent trends, with the UN working with regional organizations to provide peacekeeping assistance and humanitarian aid, are also aiding in making relief efforts in Africa more effective.

Finally, the United Nations can play a role in assisting not only those in crisis on the global periphery, but also in aiding the great powers in preventing war. Contrary to its critics, the United Nations is not a world government, nor is it likely to become one anytime soon. It possesses no sovereign territory, has no standing army, and no means of generating its own sources of revenue. Its success or failure is contingent upon the support, leadership, and cooperation of its membership. The UN is a political body. It cannot exist separately from the aims and goals of its member states. Thus the UN has often been in the cross-hairs of the great powers. First the USSR and, later, the US, withheld substantial portions of their assessments to the UN. Soviet domination of Eastern Europe, and its interventions in Hungary and Czechoslovakia, were affronts to principles in the UN Charter, as were US actions in the Western Hemisphere, most particularly in Guatemala, Nicaragua, Cuba, and the Dominican Republic. The Soviet Union remained hostile toward the UN from the time of the Korean War, through the Congo crisis, until the rise of Gorbachev signaled a change. Likewise, the United States has largely been in opposition since the late 1960s. It has issued vetoes with increasing frequency since 1970, provoking deep divisions within the UN over such matters as Nicaragua, the Arab-Israeli conflict, South Africa and, more recently, Iraq. Even France and Britain have had problems with the UN, most memorably over their invasion of Egypt in 1956, but also over their support for white rule in southern Africa. The exclusion of mainland China from the UN between 1949 and 1971 led to many problems and may have intensified the Cold War in Asia. In retrospect, China's exclusion may explain why the Cold War so often became hot in Asia, resulting in US interventions in Korea, Vietnam, Cambodia, and Laos, and the deaths of many millions of Asian peoples during the quarter century between 1950 and 1975.

The world has changed profoundly since 1945, nowhere as much as in the former colonial world. But, while the age of traditional colonialism is clearly dead, the temptations of empire persist. Curiously, despite a growing appreciation of the devastation wrought by imperialism, it has a continuing allure. Some have called for the United States to embark upon the path of neo-imperialism, where it could use its military power to impose "order" on an unruly world. There is renewed nostalgia for empire, but in the real world of the modern United Nations, as opposed to the world of imperial myth-making, it is increasingly understood that imperialism *created* many of the problems and crises the international community is struggling with today. Many of the supposed virtues of imperialism are merely the *ex post facto* rationales put forward by imperial powers throughout history, such as the civilizing mission, the search for security, even shouldering Kipling's "White Man's Burden."

The historical record warrants a skeptical attitude toward seeing the United Nations as the solution to all of the world's problems, but it also should provide a cautionary tale to those who embrace the myths of unilateralism and renewed empire. Legitimacy is paramount now, and will increasingly be so in the future. The United Nations has survived these past 60 years, in part, because of its legitimacy. The strong cannot easily use their power in ways not perceived as legitimate by the rest of the international community, and any state that seeks to do so risks misreading of the most important change in the international system in the past six decades: the discrediting and demise of the colonial world and the emergence of a new world of nearly 200 nation states. The United Nations has not only provided a structural alternative to increased imperialism over the past 60 years, it can continue to do so by offering the great powers alternatives to imperialism. Events in both Afghanistan and Iraq may yet prove to be tests of whether the great powers will accept the idea that legitimacy cannot be imposed from above.

The noted diplomatic historian A. J. P. Taylor has written that so "long as states admit no restriction of their sovereignty, wars will occur between them—some wars by design, more by miscalculation." The United Nations can thus serve to reduce some of the "chance" in relations among states. The Security Council has authorized war only twice, first in the Korean crisis of 1950 (albeit under the unique circumstances of a Soviet walkout) and during the Gulf crisis of 1990–91, demonstrating how difficult it has been to achieve consensus on the use of force. While this has been derided as a chief weakness of the UN system, in fact it reveals the extent to which many wars are avoidable. The problem is—as the most recent war in Iraq has revealed—not everyone has an interest in *avoiding* war.

One of the major challenges the United Nations is likely to face in the decades ahead is how its membership—and particularly the permanent members of the Security Council—will adjust to the profound changes that will occur in the international system. The US will, for some time, continue to press advantages conferred by its military strength. But its economic and political power may face challenges owing to the reemergence of China as a world power, the expansion and increasing relevance of the European Union, and the increasing pluralism of the new world order that has already arrived. This will require creative diplomacy of the highest order. The dawning of the nuclear age, once used as a rationale to explain the UN's irrelevance, has also demonstrated the very necessity of international institutions to aid in the resolution of conflict and the avoidance of war.

PART II

DOCUMENTS

DOCUMENT NO. 1

PRESIDENT WOODROW WILSON'S FOURTEEN POINTS[1]

The Fourteen Points, proclaimed by President Woodrow Wilson at the be-
ginning of the last year of World War I for the reordering of world politics
in the postwar era, served as the basis for negotiations at the peace conference
in 1919. The fourteenth point, calling for a "general association of nations
for the purpose of affording mutual guarantees of political independence and
territorial integrity to great and small states alike" was the inspiration for
the League of Nations.

γ γ γ

January 8, 1918

It will be our wish and purpose that the processes of peace, when they are begun, shall be absolutely open and that they shall involve and permit henceforth no secret understandings of any kind. The day of conquest and aggrandizement is gone by; so is also the day of secret covenants entered into in the interest of particular governments and likely at some unlooked-for moment to upset the peace of the world. It is this happy fact, now clear to the view of every public man whose thoughts do not still linger in an age that is dead and gone, which makes it possible for every nation whose purposes are consistent with justice and the peace of the world to avow nor or at any other time the objects it has in view.

We entered this war because violations of right had occurred which touched us to the quick and made the life of our own people impossible unless they were corrected and the world secure once and for all against their recurrence. What we demand in this war, therefore, is nothing peculiar to ourselves. It is that the world be made fit and safe to live in; and particularly that it be made safe for every peace-loving nation which, like our own, wishes to live its own life, determine its own institutions, be assured of justice and fair dealing by the other peoples of the

1. Arthur S. Link et al., eds. *The Papers of Woodrow Wilson*, vol. 45 (Princeton: Princeton University Press, 1984), 536.

world as against force and selfish aggression. All the peoples of the world are in effect partners in this interest, and for our own part we see very clearly that unless justice be done to others it will not be done to us. The programme of the world's peace, therefore, is our programme; and that programme, the only possible programme, as we see it, is this:

I. Open covenants of peace, openly arrived at, after which there shall be no private international understandings of any kind but diplomacy shall proceed always frankly and in the public view.

II. Absolute freedom of navigation upon the seas, outside territorial waters, alike in peace and in war, except as the seas may be closed in whole or in part by international action for the enforcement of international covenants.

III. The removal, so far as possible, of all economic barriers and the establishment of an equality of trade conditions among all the nations consenting to the peace and associating themselves for its maintenance.

IV. Adequate guarantees given and taken that national armaments will be reduced to the lowest point consistent with domestic safety.

V. A free, open-minded, and absolutely impartial adjustment of all colonial claims, based upon a strict observance of the principle that in determining all such questions of sovereignty the interests of the populations concerned must have equal weight with the equitable claims of the government whose title is to be determined.

VI. The evacuation of all Russian territory and such a settlement of all questions affecting Russia as will secure the best and freest cooperation of the other nations of the world in obtaining for her an unhampered and unembarrassed opportunity for the independent determination of her own political development and national policy and assure her of a sincere welcome into the society of free nations under institutions of her own choosing; and, more than a welcome, assistance also of every kind that she may need and may herself desire. The treatment accorded Russia by her sister nations in the months to come will be the acid test of their good will, of their comprehension of her needs as distinguished from their own interests, and of their intelligent and unselfish sympathy.

VII. Belgium, the whole world will agree, must be evacuated and restored, without any attempt to limit the sovereignty which she enjoys in common with all other free nations. No other single act will serve as this will serve to restore confidence among the nations in the laws which they have themselves set and determined for the government of their relations with one another. Without this healing act the whole structure and validity of international law is forever impaired.

VIII. All French territory should be freed and the invaded portions restored, and the wrong done to France by Prussia in 1871 in the matter of Alsace-Lorraine, which has unsettled the peace of the world for nearly fifty years, should be righted, in order that peace may once more be made secure in the interest of all.

IX. A readjustment of the frontiers of Italy should be effected along clearly recognizable lines of nationality.

X. The peoples of Austria-Hungary, whose place among the nations we wish to see safeguarded and assured, should be accorded the freest opportunity to autonomous development.

XI. Rumania, Serbia, and Montenegro should be evacuated; occupied territories restored; Serbia accorded free and secure access to the sea; and the relations of the several Balkan states to one another determined by friendly counsel along historically established lines of allegiance and nationality; and international guarantees of the political and economic independence and territorial integrity of the several Balkan states should be entered into.

XII. The Turkish portion of the present Ottoman Empire should be assured a secure sovereignty, but the other nationalities which are now under Turkish rule should be assured an undoubted security of life and an absolutely unmolested opportunity of autonomous development, and the Dardanelles should be permanently opened as a free passage to the ships and commerce of all nations under international guarantees.

XIII. An independent Polish state should be erected which should include the territories inhabited by indisputably Polish populations, which should be assured a free and secure access to the sea, and whose political and economic independence and territorial integrity should be guaranteed by international covenant.

XIV. A general association of nations must be formed under specific covenants for the purpose of affording mutual guarantees of political independence and territorial integrity to great and small states alike.

In regard to these essential rectifications of wrong and assertions of right we feel ourselves to be intimate partners of all the governments and peoples associated together against the Imperialists. We cannot be separated in interest or divided in purpose. We stand together until the end.

For such arrangements and covenants we are willing to fight and to continue to fight until they are achieved; but only because we wish the right to prevail and desire a just and stable peace such as can be secured only by removing the chief provocations to war, which this programme does remove. We have no jealousy of German greatness, and there is nothing in this programme that impairs it. We grudge her no achievement or distinction of learning or of pacific enterprise such as have made her record very bright and very enviable. We do not wish to injure her or to block in any way her legitimate influence or power. We do not wish to fight her either with arms or with hostile arrangements of trade if she is willing to associate herself with us and the other peace-loving nations of the world in covenants of justice and law and fair dealing. We wish her only to accept a place of equality among the peoples of the world,— the new world in which we now live,—instead of a place of mastery.

DOCUMENT NO. 2

PREAMBLE TO THE COVENANT OF THE LEAGUE OF NATIONS[2]

The Covenant of the League of Nations served as a preamble explaining the essentials of what the member nations—or "High Contracting Parties"—were committing themselves to as members of the new world organization.

2. Arthur S. Link et al., eds., *The Papers of Woodrow Wilson*, vol. 60 (Princeton: Princeton University Press, 1989), 164–178.

Despite its many failures, the League represented a remarkable experiment in transforming the relations among states.

γ   γ   γ

June 28, 1919

THE HIGH CONTRACTING PARTIES,

In order to promote international cooperation and to achieve international peace and security

by the acceptance of obligations not to resort to war,

by the prescription of open, just and honorable relations between nations,

by the firm establishment of the understandings of international law as the actual rule of conduct among Governments, and

by the maintenance of justice and a scrupulous respect for all treaty obligations in the dealings of organized peoples with one another,

Agree to this Covenant of the League of Nations.

DOCUMENT NO. 3

THE LEAGUE OF NATIONS COVENANT AND THE QUESTION OF SANCTIONS[3]

Article 16 of the League of Nations Covenant explained how members of the League could impose economic sanctions against any state that resorts to war in violation of the Covenant. It also provided for the possible expulsion of such transgressors.

γ   γ   γ

ARTICLE 16

Should any Member of the League resort to war in disregard of its covenants under Articles 12, 13 or 15, it shall ipso facto be deemed to have committed an act of war against all other Members of the League, which hereby undertake immediately to subject it to the severance of all

---

3. Arthur S. Link et al., eds., *The Papers of Woodrow Wilson*, vol. 60 (Princeton: Princeton University Press, 1989), 164–178.

trade or financial relations, the prohibition of all intercourse between their nationals and the nationals of the covenant-breaking State, and the prevention of all financial, commercial or personal intercourse between the nationals of the covenant-breaking State and the nationals of any other State, whether a Member of the League or not.

It shall be the duty of the Council in such case to recommend to the several Governments concerned what effective military, naval or air force the Members of the League shall severally contribute to the armed forces to be used to protect the covenants of the League.

The Members of the League agree, further, that they will mutually support one another in the financial and economic measures which are taken under this Article, in order to minimize the loss and inconvenience resulting from the above measures, and that they will mutually support one another in resisting any special measures aimed at one of their number by the covenant-breaking State, and that they will take the necessary steps to afford passage through their territory to the forces of any of the Members of the League which are cooperating to protect the covenants of the League.

Any Member of the League which has violated any covenant of the League may be declared to be no longer a Member of the League by a vote of the Council concurred in by the Representatives of all the other Members of the League represented thereon.

DOCUMENT NO. 4

THE ATLANTIC CHARTER, 1941[4]

This Anglo-American declaration was agreed upon nearly four months before American entry into World War II. The American President, Franklin D. Roosevelt, and the British Prime Minister, Winston Churchill, agreed to the Atlantic Charter after several days of deliberations at sea off the coast of Newfoundland. The declaration's final point, calling for "the establish-

---

4. *Yearbook of the United Nations, 1946–47* (Lake Success, NY: United Nations Office of Public Information, 1947), 1.

ment of a wider and permanent system of general security," was seen by many as pointing in the direction of reestablishing a world organization.

γ   γ   γ

August 14, 1941

The President of the United States of America and the Prime Minister, Mr. Churchill, representing His Majesty's Government in the United Kingdom, being met together, deem it right to make known certain common principles in the national policies of their respective countries on which they base their hopes for a better future for the world.

First, their countries seek no aggrandizement, territorial or other;

Second, they desire to see no territorial changes that do not accord with the freely expressed wishes of the peoples concerned;

Third, they respect the right of all peoples to choose the form of government under which they will live; and they wish to see sovereign rights and self government restored to those who have been forcibly deprived of them;

Fourth, they will endeavor, with due respect for their existing obligations, to further the enjoyment by all States, great or small, victor or vanquished, of access, on equal terms, to the trade and to the raw materials of the world which are needed for their economic prosperity;

Fifth, they desire to bring about the fullest collaboration between all nations in the economic field with the object of securing, for all, improved labor standards, economic advancement and social security;

Sixth, after the final destruction of the Nazi tyranny, they hope to see established a peace which will afford to all nations the means of dwelling in safety within their own boundaries, and which will afford assurance that all the men in all lands may live out their lives in freedom from fear and want;

Seventh, such a peace should enable all men to traverse the high seas and oceans without hindrance;

Eighth, they believe that all of the nations of the world, for realistic as well as spiritual reasons must come to the abandonment of the use of force. Since no future peace can be maintained if land, sea or air armaments continue to be employed by nations which threaten, or may threaten, aggression outside of their frontiers, they believe, pending the establishment of a wider and permanent system of general security, that the disarmament of such nations is essential. They will likewise aid and encourage all other practicable measure which will lighten for peace-loving peoples the crushing burden of armaments.

Franklin D. Roosevelt

Winston S. Churchill

DOCUMENT NO. 5

THE DECLARATION BY THE UNITED NATIONS, 1942[5]

With this declaration of January 1, 1942, the term "United Nations" emerged to identify the allied nations. The forty-seven signatories pledged to uphold the principles enunciated in the Atlantic Charter, which pledged the allies to establish a "system of general security"—interpreted to mean a new world organization. The first four signatories represented Roosevelt's concept of the Four Policemen—the United States, the United Kingdom, the USSR, and China—what would become four of the five (along with France) permanent members of the United Nations Security Council. At the San Francisco Conference in 1945 the participating nations unanimously adopted the name "United Nations" as a tribute to the recently deceased Roosevelt.

γ   γ   γ

January 1, 1942

A Joint Declaration by the United States, the United Kingdom, the Union of Soviet Socialist Republics, China, Australia, Belgium, Can-

5. *Yearbook of the United Nations, 1946–47* (Lake Success, NY: United Nations Office of Public Information, 1947), 1–2.

ada, Costa Rica, Cuba, Czechoslovakia, Dominican Republic, El Salvador, Greece, Guatemala, Haiti, Honduras, India, Luxembourg, Netherlands, New Zealand, Nicaragua, Norway, Panama, Poland, South Africa, Yugoslavia.

The Governments signatory hereto,

Having subscribed to a common program of purposes and principles embodied in the Joint Declaration of the President of the United States of America and the Prime Minister of the United Kingdom of Great Britain and Northern Ireland dated August 14, 1941, known as the Atlantic Charter.

Being convinced that complete victory over their enemies is essential to defend life, liberty, independence and religious freedom, and to preserve human rights and justice in their own lands as well as in other lands, and that they are now engaged in a common struggle against savage and brutal forces seeking to subjugate the world,

DECLARE:

(1) Each Government pledges itself to employ its full resources, military or economic, against those members of the Tripartite Pact: and its adherents with which such government is at war.

(2) Each Government pledges itself to cooperate with the Governments signatory hereto and not to make a separate armistice or peace with the enemies.

The foregoing declaration may be adhered to by other nations which are, or which may be, rendering material assistance and contributions in the struggle for victory over Hitlerism.

Done at Washington

January First, 1942

[The signatories to the Declaration by United Nations are as listed above.]

The adherents to the Declaration by United Nations, together with the date of communication of adherence, are as follows:

Mexico June 5, 1942	Peru Feb. 11, 1945
Philippines June 10, 1942	Chile Feb. 12, 1945
Ethiopia July 28, 1942	Paraguay Feb. 12, 1945
Iraq Jan. 16, 1943	Venezuela Feb. 16, 1945
Brazil Feb. 8, 1943	Uruguay Feb. 23, 1945
Bolivia Apr. 27, 1943	Turkey Feb. 24, 1945
Iran Sept. 10, 1943	Egypt Feb. 27, 1945
Colombia Dec. 22, 1943	Saudi Arabia Mar. 1, 1945
Liberia Feb. 26, 1944	Lebanon Mar. 1, 1945
France Dec. 26, 1944	Syria Mar. 1, 1945
Ecuador Feb. 7, 1945	

DOCUMENT NO. 6

DUMBARTON OAKS PROPOSALS FOR AN INTERNATIONAL ORGANIZATION[6]

At the Dumbarton Oaks Conference in Washington the four major allies discussed issues related to the creation of a new world organization. The resulting documents, the Dumbarton Oaks Proposals, owed much to the previous two years of American postwar planning, and served as the basis for the United Nations Charter. The proposals focused on a security council, an assembly, a world court, and a secretariat. Included here are excerpts explaining the purposes and principles of a new world organization.

γ   γ   γ

October 7, 1944

There should be established an international organization under the title of The United Nations, the Charter of which should contain provisions necessary to give effect to the proposals which follow.

6. *Yearbook of the United Nations, 1946–47* (Lake Success, NY: United Nations Office of Public Information, 1947), 4–9.

CHAPTER I

PURPOSES

The purposes of the Organization should be:

1. To maintain international peace and security; and to that end to take effective collective measures for the prevention and removal of threats to the peace and the suppression of acts of aggression or other breaches of the peace, and to bring about by peaceful means adjustment or settlement of international disputes which may lead to a breach of the peace;

2. To develop friendly relations among nations and to take other appropriate measures to strengthen universal peace;

3. To achieve international cooperation in the solution of international economic, social and other humanitarian problems; and

4. To afford a centre for harmonizing the actions of nations in the achievement of these common ends.

CHAPTER II

PRINCIPLES

In pursuit of the purposes mentioned in Chapter I the Organization and its members should act in accordance with the following principles:

1. The Organization is based on the principle of the sovereign equality of all peace-loving states.

2. All members of the Organization undertake, in order to ensure to all of them the rights and benefits resulting from membership in the Organization, to fulfill the obligations assumed by them in accordance with the Charter.

3. All members of the Organization shall settle their disputes by peaceful means in such a manner that international peace and security are not endangered.

4. All members of the Organization shall refrain in their international relations from the threat or use of force in any manner inconsistent with the purposes of the Organization.

5. All members of the Organization shall give every assistance to the Organization in any action undertaken by it in accordance with the provisions of the Charter.

6. All members of the Organization shall refrain from giving assistance to any state against which preventive or enforcement action is being undertaken by the Organization.

The Organization should ensure that states not members of the Organization act in accordance with these principles so far as may be necessary for the maintenance of international peace and security.

DOCUMENT NO. 7

PURPOSES OF THE WORLD BANK[7]

Prior to the Dumbarton Oaks Conference, a conference on creating a new international financial system was held at Bretton Woods, New Hampshire. Representatives from 44 nations established blueprints for the creation of international economic institutions as part of the United Nations system including the International Bank for Reconstruction and Development (the World Bank) and the International Monetary Fund (IMF). The following excerpt is from the "Articles of Agreement of the International Bank for Reconstruction and Development" and explains the purposes and functions of the World Bank.

γ   γ   γ

The Bretton Woods Agreements
Articles of Agreement of the International Bank for
Reconstruction and Development, July 22, 1944

The Governments on whose behalf the present Agreement is signed agree as follows:

INTRODUCTORY ARTICLE

The International Bank for Reconstruction and Development is established and shall operate in accordance with the following provisions:

7. *Yearbook of the United Nations, 1946–47* (Lake Success, NY: United Nations Office of Public Information, 1947), 747–766.

ARTICLE I. PURPOSES

The purposes of the Bank are:

(i) To assist in the reconstruction and development of territories of members by facilitating the investment of capital for productive purposes, including the restoration of economies destroyed or disrupted by war, the reconversion of productive facilities to peacetime needs and the encouragement of the development of productive facilities and resources in less developed countries.

(ii) To promote private foreign investment by means of guarantees or participations in loans and other investments made by private investors; and when private capital is not available on reasonable terms, to supplement private investment by providing, on suitable conditions, finance for productive purposes out of its own capital, funds raised by it and its other resources.

(iii) To promote the long-range balanced growth of international trade and the maintenance of equilibrium in balances of payments by encouraging international investment for the development of the productive resources of members, thereby assisting in raising productivity, the standard of living and conditions of labor in their territories.

(iv) To arrange the loans made or guaranteed by it in relation to international loans through other channels so that the more useful and urgent projects, large and small alike, will be dealt with first.

(v) To conduct its operations with due regard to the effect of international investment on business conditions in the territories of members and, in the immediate postwar years, to assist in bringing about a smooth transition from a wartime to a peacetime economy.

The Bank shall be guided in all its decisions by the purposes set forth above.

DOCUMENT NO. 8

PURPOSES OF THE INTERNATIONAL MONETARY FUND[8]

Another result of the Bretton Woods Conference was the establishment of an International Monetary Fund (IMF) to promote monetary stability and prevent currency fluctuations. The following excerpt, also from the "Articles of Agreement of the International Bank for Reconstruction and Development," explains the purposes and functions of the IMF.

γ   γ   γ

The Bretton Woods Agreements, July 22, 1944
The International Monetary Fund is established and shall operate in accordance with the following provisions:

ARTICLE I. PURPOSES

The purposes of the International Monetary Fund are:

(i) To promote international monetary cooperation through a permanent institution which provides the machinery for consultation and collaboration on international monetary problems.

(ii) To facilitate the expansion and balanced growth of international trade, and to contribute thereby to the promotion and maintenance of high levels of employment and real income and to the development of the productive resources of all members as primary objectives of economic policy.

(iii) To promote exchange stability, to maintain orderly exchange arrangements among members, and to avoid competitive exchange depreciation.

(iv) To assist in the establishment of a multilateral system of payments in respect of current transactions between members and in the elimi-

8. *Yearbook of the United Nations, 1946–47* (Lake Success, NY: United Nations Office of Public Information, 1947), 767–788.

nation of foreign exchange restrictions which hamper the growth of world trade.

(v) To give confidence to members by making the Fund's resources available to them under adequate safeguards, thus providing them with opportunity to correct maladjustments in their balance of payments without resorting to measures destructive of national or international prosperity.

(vi) In accordance with the above, to shorten the duration and lessen the degree of disequilibrium. in the international balances of payments of members.

The Fund shall be guided in all its decisions by the purposes set forth in this Article.

DOCUMENT NO. 9

PREAMBLE TO THE UN CHARTER[9]

The Preamble for the United Nations, in contrast to the Covenant of the League of Nations, resembles the United States Constitution in claiming that "the Peoples" have resolved to accomplish certain aims, although the representatives of specific states actually signed the Charter. In addition to uniting to maintain peace and security, other goals included the reaffirmation and furthering of fundamental human rights and the promotion of economic and social advancement.

γ   γ   γ

June 26, 1945

WE THE PEOPLES OF THE UNITED NATIONS DETER-MINED to save succeeding generations from the scourge of war, which twice in our lifetime has brought untold sorrow to mankind, and to reaffirm faith in fundamental human rights, in the dignity and worth of

9. *Yearbook of the United Nations, 1946–47* (Lake Success, NY: United Nations Office of Public Information, 1947), 831–850.

the human person, in the equal rights of men and women and of nations large and small, and to establish conditions under which justice and respect for the obligations arising from treaties and other sources of international law can be maintained, and to promote social progress and better standards of life in larger freedom, AND FOR THESE ENDS to practice tolerance and live together in peace with one another as good neighbors, and to unite our strength to maintain international peace and security, and to ensure, by the acceptance of principles and the institution of methods, that armed force shall not be used, save in the common interest, and to employ international machinery for the promotion of the economic and social advancement of all peoples, HAVE RESOLVED TO COMBINE OUR EFFORTS TO ACCOMPLISH THESE AIMS. Accordingly, our respective Governments, through representatives assembled in the city of San Francisco, who have exhibited their full powers found to be in good and due form, have agreed to the present Charter of the United Nations and do hereby establish an international organization to be known as the United Nations.

DOCUMENT NO. 10

CHAPTER VII OF THE UN CHARTER ON PEACE AND SECURITY[10]

While Chapters I through VI (Articles 1 through 38) of the United Nations Charter cover organizational and procedural matters, Chapter VII (Articles 39 through 51) focuses on threats to the peace. It features a range of measures available to the Security Council to maintain or restore peace with the possible use of force. The war which began when North Korean forces crossed the 38th parallel on June 25, 1950 marked the first time that the United Nations invoked Chapter VII to authorize force.

γ   γ   γ

CHAPTER VII of the United Nations Charter:
ACTION WITH RESPECT TO THREATS TO THE PEACE, BREACHES OF THE PEACE, AND ACTS OF AGGRESSION

10. *Yearbook of the United Nations, 1946–47* (Lake Success, NY: United Nations Office of Public Information, 1947), 835–837.

Article 39

The Security Council shall determine the existence of any threat to the peace, breach of the peace, or act of aggression and shall make recommendations, or decide what measures shall be taken in accordance with Articles 4 and 42, to maintain or restore international peace and security.

Article 40

In order to prevent an aggravation of the situation, the Security Council may, before making the recommendations or deciding upon the measures provided for in Article 39, call upon the parties concerned to comply with such provisional measures as it deems necessary or desirable. Such provisional measures shall be without prejudice to the rights, claims, or position of the parties concerned. The Security Council shall duly take account of failure to comply with such provisional measures.

Article 41

The Security Council may decide what measures not involving the use of armed force are to be employed to give effect to its decisions, and it may call upon the Members of the United Nations to apply such measures. These may include complete or partial interruption of economic relations and of rail, sea, air, postal, telegraphic, radio, and other means of communication, and the severance of diplomatic relations.

Article 42

Should the Security Council consider that measures provided for in Article 41 would be inadequate or have proved to be inadequate, it may take such action by air, sea, or land forces as may be necessary to maintain or restore international peace and security. Such action may include demonstrations, blockade, and other operations by air, sea, or land forces of Members of the United Nations.

Article 43

1. All Members of the United Nations, in order to contribute to the maintenance of international peace and security, undertake to make

available to the Security Council, on its and in accordance with a special agreement or agreements, armed forces, assistance, and facilities, including rights of passage, necessary for the purpose of maintaining international peace and security.

2. Such agreement or agreements shall govern the numbers and types of forces, their degree of readiness and general location, and the nature of the facilities and assistance to be provided.

3. The agreement or agreements shall be negotiated as soon as possible on the initiative of the Security Council. They shall be concluded between the Security Council and Members or between the Security Council and groups of Members and shall be subject to ratification by the signatory states in accordance with their respective constitutional processes.

Article 44

When Security Council has decided to use force it shall, before calling upon a Member not represented on it to provide armed forces in fulfillment of the obligations assumed under Article 43, invite that Member, if the Member so desires, to participate in the decisions of the Security Council concerning the employment of contingents of that Member's armed forces.

Article 45

In order to enable the Nations to take urgent military measures, Members shall hold immediately available national air-force contingents for combined international enforcement action. The strength and degree of readiness of these contingents and plans for their combined action shall be determined, within the limits laid down in the special agreement or agreements referred to in Article 43, by the Security Council with the assistance of the Military Committee.

Article 46

Plans for the application of armed force shall be made by the Security Council with the assistance of the Military Staff Committee.

Article 47

1. There shall be established a Military Staff Committee to advise and assist the Security Council on questions relating to the Security Council's military requirements for the maintenance of international peace and security, the employment and command of forces placed at its disposal, the regulation of armaments, and possible disarmament.

2. The Military Staff Committee consists of the Chiefs of Staff of the permanent members of the Security Council or their representatives. Any Member of the United Nations not permanently represented on the Committee shall be invited by the Committee to be associated with it when the efficient discharge of the Committee's responsibilities requires the participation of that Member its work.

3. The Military Staff Committee be responsible under the Security Council for the strategic direction of any armed forces paced at the disposal of the Security Council. Questions relating to the command of such forces shall be worked out subsequently.

4. The Military Staff Committee, with the authorization of the security Council and after consultation with appropriate regional agencies, may establish subcommittees.

Article 48

1. The action required to carry out the decisions of the Security Council for the maintenance of international peace and security shall be taken by all the Members of the United Nations or by some of them, as the Security Council may determine.

2. Such decisions shall be carried out by the Members of the United Nations directly and through their action in the appropriate international agencies of which they are members.

Article 49

The Members of the United Nations shall join in affording mutual assistance in carrying out the measures decided upon by the Security Council.

Article 50

If preventive or enforcement measures against any state are taken by the
Security Council, any other state, whether a Member of the United Nations or not, which finds itself confronted with special economic problems arising from the carrying out of those measures shall have the
right to consult the Security Council with regard to a solution of those
problems.

Article 51

Nothing in the present Charter shall impair the inherent right of individual or collective self-defense if an armed attack occurs against a
Member of the United Nations, until the Security Council has taken
measures necessary to maintain international peace and security. Measures taken by Members in the exercise of this right of self-defense shall
be immediately reported to the Security Council and shall not in any
way affect the authority and responsibility of the Security Council under the present Charter to take at any time such action as it deems necessary in order to maintain or restore international peace and security.

DOCUMENT NO. 11

ENHANCING THE POWERS OF THE GENERAL ASSEMBLY, 1950[11]

*An important development in the history of the United Nations was the
passage of the Uniting for Peace Resolution in 1950, which allowed for the
calling of an emergency session of the General Assembly if the Security
Council was deadlocked. One inherent weakness of the Security Council is
the barrier to decisive action when a stalemate is created by the use of, or the
threat to use, the veto. The "Uniting for Peace" Resolution of November 3,
1950 amounted to an informal amendment of the Charter and demonstrated
the flexibility of the institution to adjust to new challenges. In the midst*

11. *Yearbook of the United Nations, 1950* (New York: Columbia University Press, 1951),
193–195.

of the Korean War this innovative mechanism was used to circumvent the stalemate on the Security Council. Here, the General Assembly stepped in and assumed the legal authority for the use of force—something previously thought to be within the sole jurisdiction of the Security Council.

γ   γ   γ

Uniting for Peace
Excerpts from United Nations General Assembly Resolution 377(V)
November 3, 1950

The General Assembly,

Recognizing that the first two stated Purposes of the United Nations are:

"To maintain international peace and security, and to that end: to take effective collective measures for the prevention and removal of threats to the peace, and for the suppression of acts of aggression or other breaches of the peace, and to bring about by peaceful means, and in conformity with the principles of justice and international law, adjustment or settlement of international disputes or situations which might lead to a breach of the peace", and

"To develop friendly relations among nations based on respect for the principle of equal rights and self-determination of peoples, and to take other appropriate measures to strengthen universal peace",
Reaffirming that it remains the primary duty of all Members of the United Nations, when involved in an international dispute, to seek settlement of such a dispute by peaceful means through the procedures laid down in Chapter VI of the Charter, and recalling the successful achievements of the United Nations in this regard on a number of previous occasions,

Finding that international tension exists on a dangerous scale,

Recalling its resolution 290 (IV) entitled "Essentials of peace", which states that disregard of the Principles of the Charter of the United Nations is primarily responsible for the continuance of international tension, and desiring to contribute further to the objectives of that resolution,

Reaffirming the importance of the exercise by the Security Council of its primary responsibility for the maintenance of international peace and security, and the duty of the permanent members to seek unanimity and to exercise restraint in the use of the veto,

Reaffirming that the initiative in negotiating the agreements for armed forces provided for in Article 43 of the Charter belongs to the Security Council, and desiring to ensure that, pending the conclusion of such agreements, the United Nations has at its disposal means for maintaining international peace and security,

Conscious that failure of the Security Council to discharge its responsibilities on behalf of all the Member States, particularly those responsibilities referred to in the two preceding paragraphs, does not relieve Member States of their obligations or the United Nations of its responsibility under the Charter to maintain international peace and security,

Recognizing in particular that such failure does not deprive the General Assembly of its rights or relieve it of its responsibilities under the Charter in regard to the maintenance of international peace and security,

Recognizing that discharge by the General Assembly of its responsibilities in these respects calls for possibilities of observation which would ascertain the facts and expose aggressors; for the existence of armed forces which could be used collectively; and for the possibility of timely recommendation by the General Assembly to Members of the United Nations for collective action which, to be effective, should be prompt,

A

1. Resolves that if the Security Council, because of lack of unanimity of the permanent members, fails to exercise its primary responsibility for the maintenance of international peace and security in any case where there appears to be a threat to the peace, breach of the peace, or act of aggression, the General Assembly shall consider the matter immediately with a view to making appropriate recommendations to Members for collective measures, including in the case of a breach of the peace or act of aggression the use of armed force when necessary, to maintain or restore international peace and security. If not in session at

the time, the General Assembly may meet in emergency special session within twenty-four hours of the request therefor. Such emergency special session shall be called if requested by the Security Council on the vote of any seven members, or by a majority of the Members of the United Nations;

2. Adopts for this purpose the amendments to its rules of procedure set forth in the annex to the present resolution. . . .

302nd plenary meeting
3 November 1950

DOCUMENT NO. 12

WORLD COURT DECISION ON *NICARAGUA V. USA*, 1986[12]

In the final years of the Cold War the United States backed an insurgency in the Central American nation of Nicaragua—the Contra rebels—aimed to pressure, and perhaps overthrow, the Sandinista regime. The US also mined harbors and launched other covert operations to destabilize the Nicaraguan economy. Nicaragua successfully lodged a series of complaints at the UN against US actions and also before the International Court of Justice, charging the United States with violations of its sovereignty. The US vetoed seven Resolutions critical of its actions toward Nicaragua. As shown in the following excerpt, in 1986 the International Court of Justice (the World Court) ruled in Nicaragua's favor on 16 counts. The United States refused to recognize the jurisdiction of the World Court or the validity of its verdicts, despite the fact that it had signed the so-called "optional clause" granting jurisdiction in such circumstances. After this verdict, the United States rescinded its adherence to that clause. Controversies at the UN over US policy in the region deepened the rift between the Reagan administration and the United Nations during the 1980s.

γ   γ   γ

12. The International Court of Justice's opinion can be obtained in its entirety at its website: http://212.153.43.18/icjwww/icases/inus/inusframe.htm

International Court of Justice

CASE CONCERNING THE MILITARY AND PARAMILITARY ACTIVITIES IN AND AGAINST NICARAGUA
Judgment of 27 June 1986

For its judgment on the merits in the case concerning military and Paramilitary Activities in and against Nicaragua brought by Nicaragua against the United States of America, the Court was composed as follows:

President Nagendra Singh, Vice-President de Lacharrière; Judges Lachs, Ruda, Elias, Oda, Ago, Sette-Camara, Schwebel, Sir Robert Jennings, Mbaye, Bedjaoui, Ni, Evensen, Judge ad hoc Colliard

OPERATIVE PART OF THE COURT'S JUDGMENT

THE COURT

(1) By eleven votes to four,

Decides that in adjudicating the dispute brought before it by the Application filed by the Republic of Nicaragua on 9 April 1984, the Court is required to apply the "multilateral treaty reservation "contained in proviso (c) to the declaration of acceptance of jurisdiction made under Article 36, paragraph 2, of the Statute of the Court by the Government of the Untied States of America deposited on 26 August 1946;

IN FAVOUR: President Nagendra Singh; Vice-President de Lacharrière; Judges Lachs, Oda, Ago, Schwebel, Sir Robert Jennings, Mbaye, Bedjaoui and Evensen; Judge ad hoc Colliard;

AGAINST: Judges Ruda, Elias, Sette-Camara and Ni.

(2) By twelve votes to three,

Rejects the justification of collective self-defense maintained by the United States of America in connection with the military and paramilitary activities in and against Nicaragua the subject of this case;

IN FAVOUR: President Nagendra Singh; Vice-President de Lacharrière; Judges Lachs, Ruda, Elias, Ago, Sette-Camara, Mbaye, Bedjaoui, Ni and Evensen; Judge ad hoc Colliard;

AGAINST: Judges Oda, Schwebel and Sir Robert Jennings.

(3) By twelve votes to three,

Decides that the United States of America, by training, arming, equipping, financing and supplying the contra forces or otherwise encouraging, supporting and aiding military and paramilitary activities in and against Nicaragua, has acted, against the Republic of Nicaragua, in breach of its obligation under customary international law not to intervene in the affairs of another State;

IN FAVOUR: President Nagendra Singh; Vice-President de Lacharrière; Judges Lachs, Ruda, Elias, Ago, Sette-Camara, Mbaye, Bedjaoui, Ni and Evensen; Judge ad hoc Colliard;

AGAINST: Judges Oda, Schwebel and Sir Robert Jennings.

(4) By twelve votes to three,

Decides that the United States of America, by certain attacks on Nicaraguan territory in 1983-1984, namely attacks on Puerto Sandino on 13 September and 14 October 1983, an attack on Corinto on 10 October 1983; an attack on Potosi Naval Base on 4/5 January 1984, an attack on San Juan del Sur on 7 March 1984; attacks on patrol boats at Puerto Sandino on 28 and 30 March 1984; and an attack on San Juan del Norte on 9 April 1984; and further by those acts of intervention referred to in subparagraph (3) hereof which involve the use of force, has acted, against the Republic of Nicaragua, in breach of its obligation under customary international law not to use force against another State;

IN FAVOUR: President Nagendra Singh; Vice-President de Lacharrière; Judges Lachs, Ruda, Elias, Ago, Sette-Camara, Mbaye, Bedjaoui, Ni and Evensen; Judge ad hoc Colliard;

AGAINST: Judges Oda, Schwebel and Sir Robert Jennings.

(5) By twelve votes to three,

Decides that the United States of America, by directing or authorizing over Rights of Nicaraguan territory, and by the acts imputable to the United States referred to in subparagraph (4) hereof, has acted, against the Republic of Nicaragua, in breach of its obligation under customary international law not to violate the sovereignty of another State;

IN FAVOUR: President Nagendra Singh; Vice-President de Lacharrière; Judges Lachs, Ruda, Elias, Ago, Sette-Camara, Mbaye, Bedjaoui, Ni and Evensen; Judge ad hoc Colliard;

AGAINST: Judges Oda, Schwebel and Sir Robert Jennings.

(6) By twelve votes to three,

Decides that, by laying mines in the internal or territorial waters of the Republic of Nicaragua during the first months of 1984, the United States of America has acted, against the Republic of Nicaragua, in breach of its obligations under customary international law not to use force against another State, not to intervene in its affairs, not to violate its sovereignty and not to interrupt peaceful maritime commerce;

IN FAVOUR: President Nagendra Singh, Vice-President de Lacharrière; Judges Lachs, Ruda, Elias, Ago, Sette-Camara, Mbaye, Bedjaoui, Ni and Evensen; Judge ad hoc Colliard;

AGAINST: Judges Oda, Schwebel and Sir Robert Jennings.

(7) By fourteen votes to one,

Decides that, by the acts referred to in subparagraph (6) hereof the United States of America has acted, against the Republic of Nicaragua, in breach of its obligations under Article XIX of the Treaty of Friendship, Commerce and Navigation between the United States of America and the Republic of Nicaragua signed at Managua on 21 January 1956;

IN FAVOUR: President Nagendra Singh, Vice-President de Lacharrière; Judges Lachs, Ruda, Elias, Oda, Ago, Sette-Camara, Sir Robert Jennings, Mbaye, Bedjaoui, Ni and Evensen; Judge ad hoc Colliard;

AGAINST: Judge Schwebel.

(8) By fourteen votes to one,

Decides that the United States of America, by failing to make known the existence and location of the mines laid by it, referred to in subparagraph (6) hereof, has acted in breach of its obligations under customary international law in this respect;

IN FAVOUR: President Nagendra Singh; Vice-President de Lacharrière, Judges Lachs, Ruda, Elias, Ago, Sette Camara, Schwebel, Sir Robert Jennings, Mbaye, Bedjaoui, Ni and Evensen; Judge ad hoc Colliard;

AGAINST: Judge Oda.

(9) By fourteen votes to one,

Finds that the United States of America, by producing in 1983 a manual entitled "Operaciones sicológicas en guerra de guerrillas", and disseminating it to contra forces, has encouraged the commission by them of acts contrary to general principles of humanitarian law; but does not find a basis for concluding that any such acts which may have been committed are imputable to the United States of America as acts of the United States of America;

IN FAVOUR: President Nagendra Singh; Vice-President de Lacharrière; Judges Lachs, Ruda, Elias, Ago, Sette Camara, Schwebel, Sir Robert Jennings, Mbaye, Bedjaoui, Ni and Evensen; Judge ad hoc Colliard;

AGAINST: Judge Oda.

(10) By twelve votes to three,

Decides that the United States of America, by the attacks on Nicaraguan territory referred to in subparagraph (4) hereof, and by declaring a general embargo on trade with Nicaragua on 1 May 1985, has committed acts calculated to deprive of its object and purpose the Treaty of Friendship, Commerce and Navigation between the Parties signed at Managua on 21 January 1956;

IN FAVOUR: President Nagendra Singh; Vice-President de Lacharrière; Judges Lachs, Ruda, Elias, Ago, Sette Camara, Mbaye, Bedjaoui, Ni and Evensen; Judge ad hoc Colliard;

AGAINST: Judges Oda, Schwebel and Sir Robert Jennings.

(11) By twelve votes to three,

Decides that the United States of America, by the attacks on Nicaraguan territory referred to in subparagraph (4) hereof, and by declaring a general embargo on trade with Nicaragua on 1 May 1985, has acted in breach of its obligations under Article XIX of the Treaty of Friendship, Commerce and Navigation between the Parties signed at Managua on 21 January 1956;

IN FAVOUR: President Nagendra Singh; Vice-President de Lacharrière; Judges Lachs, Ruda, Elias, Ago, Sette-Camara, Mbaye, Bedjaoui, Ni and Evensen; Judge ad hoc Colliard;

AGAINST: Judges Oda, Schwebel and Sir Robert Jennings.

(12) By twelve votes to three,

Decides that the United States of America is under a duty immediately to cease and to refrain from all such acts as may constitute breaches of the foregoing legal obligations;

IN FAVOUR: President Nagendra Singh; Vice-President de Lacharrière; Judges Lachs, Ruda, Elias, Ago, Sette Camara, Mbaye, Bedjaoui, Ni and Evensen; Judge ad hoc Colliard;

AGAINST: Judges Oda, Schwebel and Sir Robert Jennings.

(13) By twelve votes to three,

Decides that the United States of America is under an obligation to make reparation to the Republic of Nicaragua for all injury caused to Nicaragua by the breaches of obligations under customary international law enumerated above;

IN FAVOUR: President Nagendra Singh; Vice-President de Lacharrière; Judges Lachs, Ruda, Elias, Ago, Sette-Camara, Mbaye, Bedjaoui, Ni and Evensen; Judge ad hoc Colliard;

AGAINST: Judges Oda, Schwebel and Sir Robert Jennings.

(14) By fourteen votes to one,

Decides that the United States of America is under an obligation to make reparation to the Republic of Nicaragua for all injury caused to Nicaragua by the breaches of the Treaty of Friendship, Commerce and Navigation between the Parties signed at Managua on 21 January 1956;

IN FAVOUR: President Nagendra Singh; Vice-President de Lacharrière; Judges Lachs, Ruda, Elias, Oda, Ago, Sette-Camara, Sir Robert Jennings, Mbaye, Bedjaoui, Ni and Evensen; Judge ad hoc Colliard;

AGAINST: Judge Schwebel.

(15) By fourteen votes to one,

Decides that the form and amount of such reparation, failing agreement between the Parties, will be settled by the Court, and reserves for this purpose the subsequent procedure in the case;

IN FAVOUR: President Nagendra Singh; Vice-President de Lacharrière; Judges Lachs, Ruda, Elias, Oda, Ago, Sette Camara, Sir Robert Jennings, Mbaye, Bedjaoui, Ni and Evensen; Judge ad hoc Colliard;

AGAINST: Judge Schwebel.

(16) Unanimously,

Recalls to both Parties their obligation to seek a solution to their disputes by peaceful means in accordance with international law.

DOCUMENT NO. 13

SOVIET LEADER MIKHAIL GORBACHEV PROPOSES AN END TO THE COLD WAR DURING AN ADDRESS TO THE UN, 1988[13]

During his tenure as leader of the USSR Mikhail Gorbachev envisioned the United Nations as playing a pivotal role in the revolution he was planning for Soviet foreign policy. Gorbachev addressed the United Nations in December 1988 (excerpted below) in what, in hindsight, appears to have amounted to a unilateral declaration of the end of the Cold War. He proposed that the UN should now take center stage in the international system.

γ   γ   γ

Address by Mikhail Gorbachev to the United Nations, December 7, 1988
43rd U.N. General Assembly Session

Two great revolutions, the French revolution of 1789 and the Russian revolution of 1917, have exerted a powerful influence on the actual nature of the historical process and radically changed the course of world events. Both of them, each in its own way, have given a gigantic impetus to man's progress. They are also the ones that have formed in many respects the way of thinking which is still prevailing in the public consciousness.

That is a very great spiritual wealth, but there emerges before us today a different world, for which it is necessary to seek different roads toward the future, to seek—relying, of course, on accumulated experience—but also seeing the radical differences between that which was yesterday and that which is taking place today.

The newness of the tasks, and at the same time their difficulty, are not limited to this. Today we have entered an era when progress will be based on the interests of all mankind. Consciousness of this requires that world policy, too, should be determined by the priority of the values of all mankind.

13. Excerpted from "CNN—Cold War" at: http://oll.temple.edu/hist249/course/Documents/gorbachev_speech_to_UN.htm

The history of the past centuries and millennia has been a history of almost ubiquitous wars, and sometimes desperate battles, leading to mutual destruction. They occurred in the clash of social and political interests and national hostility, be it from ideological or religious incompatibility. All that was the case, and even now many still claim that this past—which has not been overcome—is an immutable pattern. However, parallel with the process of wars, hostility, and alienation of peoples and countries, another process, just as objectively conditioned, was in motion and gaining force: The process of the emergence of a mutually connected and integral world.

Further world progress is now possible only through the search for a consensus of all mankind, in movement toward a new world order. We have arrived at a frontier at which controlled spontaneity leads to a dead end. The world community must learn to shape and direct the process in such a way as to preserve civilization, to make it safe for all and more pleasant for normal life. It is a question of cooperation that could be more accurately called "co-creation" and "co-development." The formula of development "at another's expense" is becoming outdated. In light of present realities, genuine progress by infringing upon the rights and liberties of man and peoples, or at the expense of nature, is impossible.

The very tackling of global problems requires a new "volume" and "quality" of cooperation by states and sociopolitical currents regardless of ideological and other differences.

Of course, radical and revolutionary changes are taking place and will continue to take place within individual countries and social structures. This has been and will continue to be the case, but our times are making corrections here, too. Internal transformational processes cannot achieve their national objectives merely by taking a "course parallel" with others without using the achievements of the surrounding world and the possibilities of equitable cooperation. In these conditions, interference in those internal processes with the aim of altering them according to someone else's prescription would be all the more destructive for the emergence of a peaceful order. In the past, differences often served as a factor in pulling away from one another. Now they are being given the opportunity to be a factor in mutual enrichment and attraction. Behind differences in social structure, in the way of life, and in the preference for certain values, stand interests. There is no getting away from that, but neither is there any getting away from the need to find a balance of interests within an international framework, which has become a condition for survival and progress. As you ponder all this, you come to the conclusion that if we wish to take account of the lessons of the past and the realities of the present, if we must reckon with the objective logic of world development, it is necessary to seek—and seek jointly—an approach toward improving the international situation and building a new world. If that is so, then it is also worth agreeing on the fundamental and truly universal prerequisites and principles for such activities. It is evident, for example, that force and the threat of force can no longer be, and should not be instruments of foreign policy. . . .

The compelling necessity of the principle of freedom of choice is also clear to us. The failure to recognize this, to recognize it, is fraught with very dire consequences, consequences for world peace. Denying that right to the peoples, no matter what the pretext, no matter what the words are used to conceal it, means infringing upon even the unstable balance that is, has been possible to achieve.

Freedom of choice is a universal principle to which there should be no exceptions. We have not come to the conclusion of the immutability of this principle simply through good motives. We have been led to it through impartial analysis of the objective processes of our time. The increasing varieties of social development in different countries are becoming an ever more perceptible feature of these processes. This relates to both the capitalist and socialist systems. The variety of sociopolitical structures which has grown over the last decades from national liberation movements also demonstrates this. . . .

The de-ideologization of interstate relations has become a demand of the new stage. We are not giving up our convictions, philosophy, or traditions. Neither are we calling on anyone else to give up theirs. Yet we are not going to shut ourselves up within the range of our values. That would lead to spiritual impoverishment, for it would mean renouncing so powerful a source of development as sharing all the original things created independently by each nation. In the course of such sharing, each should prove the advantages of his own system, his own way of life and values, but not through words or propaganda alone, but through real deeds as well. That is, indeed, an honest struggle of ideology, but it must not be carried over into mutual relations between states. Otherwise we simply will not be able to solve a single world problem; arrange broad, mutually advantageous and equitable cooperation between peoples; manage rationally the achievements of the scientific and technical revolution; transform world economic relations; protect the environment; overcome underdevelopment; or put an end to hunger, disease, illiteracy, and other mass ills. Finally, in that case, we will not manage to eliminate the nuclear threat and militarism.

Such are our reflections on the natural order of things in the world on the threshold of the 21st century. We are, of course, far from claiming to have infallible truth, but having subjected the previous realities—realities that have arisen again—to strict analysis, we have come to the conclusion that it is by precisely such approaches that we must search jointly for a way to achieve the supremacy of the common human idea over the countless multiplicity of centrifugal forces, to preserve the vitality of a civilization that is possible that only one in the universe. . . .

We intend to expand the Soviet Union's participation in the monitoring mechanism on human rights in the United Nations and within the framework of the pan-European process. We consider that the jurisdiction of the International Court in The Hague with respect to interpreting and applying agreements in the field of human rights should be obligatory for all states.

Within the Helsinki process, we are also examining an end to jamming of all the foreign radio broadcasts to the Soviet Union. On the whole, our credo is as follows: Political problems should be solved only by political means, and human problems only in a humane way.

Now about the most important topic, without which no problem of the coming century can be resolved: disarmament.

Today I can inform you of the following: The Soviet Union has made a decision on reducing its armed forces. In the next two years, their numerical strength will be reduced by 500,000 persons, and the volume of conventional arms will also be cut considerably. These reductions will be made on a unilateral basis, unconnected with negotiations on the mandate for the Vienna meeting. By agreement with our allies in the Warsaw Pact, we have made the decision to withdraw six tank divisions from the GDR, Czechoslovakia, and Hungary, and to disband them by 1991. Assault landing formations and units, and a number of others, including assault river-crossing forces, with their armaments and combat equipment, will also be withdrawn from the groups of Soviet forces situated in those countries. The Soviet forces situated in those countries will be cut by 50,000 persons, and their arms by 5,000 tanks. All remaining Soviet divisions on the territory of our allies will be reorganized. They will be given a different structure from today's which will become unambiguously defensive, after the removal of a large number of their tanks.

By this act, just as by all our actions aimed at the demilitarization of international relations, we would also like to draw the attention of the world community to another topical problem, the problem of changing over from an economy of armament to an economy of disarmament. Is the conversion of military production realistic? I have already had occasion to speak about this. We believe that it is, indeed, realistic. For its part, the Soviet Union is ready to do the following. Within the framework of the economic reform we are ready to draw up and submit our internal plan for conversion, to prepare in the course of 1989, as an experiment, the plans for the conversion of two or three defense enterprises, to publish our experience of job relocation of specialists from the military industry, and also of using its equipment, buildings, and works in civilian industry, It is desirable that all states, primarily the major military powers, submit their national plans on this issue to the United Nations.

It would be useful to form a group of scientists, entrusting it with a comprehensive analysis of problems of conversion as a whole and as applied to individual countries and regions, to be reported to the U.N. secretary-general, and later to examine this matter at a General Assembly session.

Finally, being on U.S. soil, but also for other, understandable reasons, I cannot but turn to the subject of our relations with this great country.

. . . Relations between the Soviet Union and the United States of America span 5 1/2 decades. The world has changed, and so have the nature, role, and place of these relations in world politics. For too long they were built under the banner of confrontation, and sometimes of hostility, either open or concealed. But in the last few years, throughout the world people were able to heave a sigh of relief, thanks to the changes for the better in the substance and atmosphere of the relations between Moscow and Washington.

No one intends to underestimate the serious nature of the disagreements, and the difficulties of the problems which have not been settled. However, we have already graduated from the primary school of instruction in mutual understanding and in searching for solutions in our and in the common interests. The U.S.S.R. and the United States created the biggest nuclear missile arsenals, but after objectively recognizing their responsibility, they were able to be the first to conclude an agreement on the reduction and physical destruction of a proportion of these weapons, which threatened both themselves and everyone else. . . .

We are talking first and foremost about consistent progress toward concluding a treaty on a 50 percent reduction in strategic offensive weapons, while retaining the ABM Treaty; about elaborating a convention on the elimination of chemical weapons—here, it seems to us, we have the preconditions for making 1989 the decisive year; and about talks on reducing conventional weapons and armed forces in Europe. We are also talking about economic, ecological and humanitarian problems in the widest possible sense.

We are not inclined to oversimplify the situation in the world. Yes, the tendency toward disarmament has received a strong impetus, and this process is gaining its own momentum, but it has not become irreversible. Yes, the striving to give up confrontation in favor of dialogue and cooperation has made itself strongly felt, but it has by no means secured its position forever in the practice of international relations. Yes, the movement toward a nuclear-free and nonviolent world is capable of fundamentally transforming the political and spiritual face of the planet, but only the very first steps have been taken. Moreover, in certain influential circles, they have been greeted with mistrust, and they are meeting resistance.

The inheritance of inertia of the past are continuing to operate. Profound contradictions and the roots of many conflicts have not disappeared. The fundamental fact remains that the formation of the peaceful period will take place in conditions of the existence and rivalry of various socioeconomic and political systems. However, the meaning of our international efforts, and one of the key tenets of the new thinking, is precisely to impart to this rivalry the quality of sensible competition in conditions of respect for freedom of choice and a balance of interests. In this case it will even become useful and productive from the viewpoint of general world development; otherwise; if the main component remains the arms race, as it has been till now, rivalry will be fatal. Indeed, an ever greater number of people throughout the world, from the man in the street to leaders, are beginning to understand this.

Esteemed Mr. Chairman, esteemed delegates: I finish my first speech at the United Nations with the same feeling with which I began it: a feeling of responsibility to my own people and to the world community. We have met at the end of a year that has been so significant for the United Nations, and on the threshold of a year from which all of us expect so much. One would like to believe that our joint efforts to put an end to the era of wars, confrontation and regional conflicts, aggression against nature, the terror of hunger and poverty, as well as political terrorism, will be comparable with our hopes. This is our common goal, and it is only by acting together that we may attain it. Thank you.

DOCUMENT NO. 14

THE DISPATCH OF UN PEACEKEEPERS TO EAST TIMOR[14]

Since 1976 the United Nations adopted annual Resolutions calling for self-determination in East Timor, which, after having been a colony of Portugal for 400 years, had been brutally invaded and annexed by neighboring Indonesia in 1975. In June of 1999 the United Nations Security Council called for a secret ballot in East Timor to determine the wishes of its people and, on August 30, 1999, with a heavy turnout, nearly 80 percent of those

---

14. This Resolution can be obtained the UN's website at http://www.un.int/usa/sres1264.htm

voting cast their ballots for independence. On September 15, 1999 the Security Council adopted Resolution 1264 establishing a multinational force to end the violence and uphold the referendum in favor of self-determination. Indonesian forces departed on November 1, 1999 and the new nation of East Timor was officially born on May 20, 2002.

γ   γ   γ

RESOLUTION 1264

Adopted by the Security Council at its 4045th meeting, on 15 September 1999

Authorizing the establishment of a Multinational Force to be dispatched to East Timor

The Security Council,

Recalling its previous resolutions and the statements of its President on the situation in East Timor,

Recalling also the Agreement between Indonesia and Portugal on the question of East Timor of 5 May 1999 and the Agreements between the United Nations and the Governments of Indonesia and Portugal of the same date regarding the modalities for the popular consultation of the East Timorese through a direct ballot and security arrangements (S/1999/513, Annexes I to III),

Reiterating its welcome for the successful conduct of the popular consultation of the East Timorese people of 30 August 1999 and taking note of its outcome, which it regards as an accurate reflection of the views of the East Timorese people,

Deeply concerned by the deterioration in the security situation in East Timor, and in particular by the continuing violence against and large-scale displacement and relocation of East Timorese civilians,

Deeply concerned also at the attacks on the staff and premises of the United Nations Mission in East Timor (UNAMET), on other officials and on international and national humanitarian personnel,

Recalling the relevant principles contained in the Convention on the Safety of United Nations and Associated Personnel adopted on 9 December 1994,

Appalled by the worsening humanitarian situation in East Timor, particularly as it affects women, children and other vulnerable groups,

Reaffirming the right of refugees and displaced persons to return in safety and security to their homes, 99–26481 (E)

Endorsing the report of the Security Council Mission to Jakarta and Dili (S/1999/976),

Welcoming the statement by the President of Indonesia on 12 September 1999 in which he expressed the readiness of Indonesia to accept an international peacekeeping force through the United Nations in East Timor,

Welcoming the letter from the Minister for Foreign Affairs of Australia to the Secretary-General of 14 September 1999 (S/1999/975),

Reaffirming respect for the sovereignty and territorial integrity of Indonesia,

Expressing its concern at reports indicating that systematic, widespread and flagrant violations of international humanitarian and human rights law have been committed in East Timor, and stressing that persons committing such violations bear individual responsibility,

Determining that the present situation in East Timor constitutes a threat to peace and security, Acting under Chapter VII of the Charter of the United Nations,

1. Condemns all acts of violence in East Timor, calls for their immediate end and demands that those responsible for such acts be brought to justice;

2. Emphasizes the urgent need for coordinated humanitarian assistance and the importance of allowing full, safe and unimpeded access by humanitarian organizations and calls upon all parties to cooperate with such organizations so as to ensure the protection of civilians at risk, the safe return of refugees and displaced persons and the effective delivery of humanitarian aid;

3. Authorizes the establishment of a multinational force under a unified command structure, pursuant to the request of the Government of Indonesia conveyed to the Secretary-General on 12 September 1999, with the following tasks: to restore peace and security in East Timor, to protect and support UNAMET in carrying out its tasks and, within force capabilities, to facilitate humanitarian assistance operations, and authorizes the States participating in the multinational force to take all necessary measures to fulfill this mandate;

4. Welcomes the expressed commitment of the Government of Indonesia to cooperate with the multinational force in all aspects of the implementation of its mandate and looks forward to close coordination between the multinational force and the Government of Indonesia;

5. Underlines the Government of Indonesia's continuing responsibility under the Agreements of 5 May 1999, taking into account the mandate of the multinational force set out in paragraph 3 above, to maintain peace and security in East Timor in the interim phase between the conclusion of the popular consultation and the start of the implementation of its result and to guarantee the security of the personnel and premises of UNAMET;

6. Welcomes the offers by Member States to organize, lead and contribute to the multinational force in East Timor, calls on Member States to make further contributions of personnel, equipment and other resources and invites Member States in a position to contribute to inform the leadership of the multinational force and the Secretary-General;

7. Stresses that it is the responsibility of the Indonesian authorities to take immediate and effective measures to ensure the safe return of refugees to East Timor;

8. Notes that Article 6 of the Agreement of 5 May 1999 states that the Governments of Indonesia and Portugal and the Secretary-General shall agree on arrangements for a peaceful and orderly transfer of authority in East Timor to the United Nations, and requests the leadership of the multinational force to cooperate closely with the United Nations to assist and support those arrangements;

9. Stresses that the expenses for the force will be borne by the participating Member States concerned and requests the Secretary-General to establish a trust fund through which contributions could be channeled to the States or operations concerned;

10. Agrees that the multinational force should collectively be deployed in East Timor until replaced as soon as possible by a United Nations peacekeeping operation, and invites the Secretary-General to make prompt recommendations on a peacekeeping operation to the Security Council;

11. Invites the Secretary-General to plan and prepare for a United Nations transitional administration in East Timor, incorporating a United Nations peacekeeping operation, to be deployed in the implementation phase of the popular consultation (phase III) and to make recommendations as soon as possible to the Security Council;

12. Requests the leadership of the multinational force to provide periodic reports on progress towards the implementation of its mandate through the Secretary-General to the Council, the first such report to be made within 14 days of the adoption of this resolution;

13. Decides to remain actively seized of the matter.

DOCUMENT NO. 15

UNITED NATIONS RECOMMENDATIONS ON PALESTINE, 1947[15]

The Palestine crisis and its aftermath became one of the UN's long-running concerns. In April 1947 the UN established the United Nations Special Committee on Palestine (UNSCOP) to search for a resolution. UNSCOP's majority recommendations, excerpted below, suggested partitioning Palestine into two separate states, whereas the minority report recommended a federated unitary state. In November 1947 this partition plan was incorporated into

15. *Yearbook of the United Nations, 1947–48* (Lake Success, NY: United Nations Office of Public Information, 1949), 227–247.

General Assembly Resolution 181. The very detailed and legalistic descriptions of the boundaries of the proposed plan of partition have been omitted from these excerpts.

γ   γ   γ

November 25, 1947

FUTURE GOVERNMENT OF PALESTINE
THE GENERAL ASSEMBLY

HAVING MET in special session at the request of the Mandatory Power to constitute and instruct a Special Committee to prepare for the consideration of the question of the future government of Palestine at the second regular session;

HAVING CONSTITUTED a Special Committee and instructed it to investigate all questions and issues relevant to the problem of Palestine, and to prepare proposals for the solution of the problem; and

HAVING RECEIVED AND EXAMINED the report of the Special Committee (document A/364) including a number of unanimous recommendations and a plan of partition with economic union approved by the majority of the Special Committee;

CONSIDERS that the present situation in Palestine is one which is likely to impair the general welfare and friendly relations among nations;

TAKES NOTE of the declaration by the Mandatory Power that it plans to complete its evacuation of Palestine by 1 August 1948;

RECOMMENDS to the United Kingdom, as the Mandatory Power for Palestine, and to all other Members of the United Nations the adoption and implementation, with regard to the future government of Palestine, of the Plan of Partition with Economic Union set out below;

REQUESTS that

(a) The Security Council take the necessary measures as provided for in the Plan for its implementation;

(b) The Security Council consider if circumstances during the transitional period require such consideration, whether the situation in Palestine constitutes a threat to the peace. If it decides that such a threat exists, and in order to maintain international peace and security, the Security Council should supplement the authorization of the General Assembly by taking measures, under Articles 39 and 41 of the Charter, to empower the United Nations Commission, as provided in this resolution, to exercise in Palestine the functions which are assigned to it by this resolution;

(c) The Security Council determine as a threat to the peace, breach of the peace or act of aggression, in accordance with Article 39 of the Charter, any attempt to alter by force the settlement envisaged by this resolution;

(d) The Trusteeship Council be informed of the responsibilities envisaged for it in this Plan;

CALLS UPON the inhabitants of Palestine to take such steps as may be necessary on their part to put this Plan into effect;

APPEALS to all Governments and all peoples to refrain from taking any action which might hamper or delay the carrying out of these recommendations; and

AUTHORIZES the Secretary-General to reimburse travel and subsistence expenses of the members of the Commission referred to in Part I, Section B, paragraph 1 below on such basis and in such form as he may determine most appropriate in the circumstances, and to provide to the Commission the necessary staff to assist in carrying out the functions assigned to the Commission by the General Assembly.

PLAN OF PARTITION WITH ECONOMIC UNION
PART I. FUTURE CONSTITUTION AND GOVERNMENT OF PALESTINE
A. TERMINATION OF MANDATE, PARTITION AND INDEPENDENCE

1. The Mandate for Palestine shall terminate as soon as possible but in any case not later than 1 August 1948.

2. The armed forces of the Mandatory Power shall be progressively withdrawn from Palestine, the withdrawal to be completed as soon as possible but in any case not later than 1 August 1948.

The Mandatory Power shall advise the Commission, as far in advance as possible, of its intention to terminate the Mandate and to evacuate each area.

The Mandatory Power shall use its best endeavors to ensure that an area situated in the territory of the Jewish State, including a seaport and hinterland adequate to provide facilities for a substantial immigration, shall be evacuated at the earliest possible date and in any event not later than 1 February 1948.

3. Independent Arab and Jewish States and the Special International Regime for the City of Jerusalem, set forth in Part III of this Plan, shall come into, existence in Palestine two months after the evacuation of the armed forces of the Mandatory Power has been completed but in any case not later than 1 October 1948. The boundaries of the Arab State, the Jewish State, and the City of Jerusalem shall be as described in Parts II and III below.

4. The period between the adoption by the General Assembly of its recommendation on the question of Palestine and the establishment of the independence of the Arab and Jewish States shall be a transitional period.

B. STEPS PREPARATORY TO INDEPENDENCE

1. A Commission shall be set up consisting of one representative of each of five Member States. The Members represented on the Commission shall be elected by the General Assembly on as broad a basis, geographically and otherwise, as possible.

2. The administration of Palestine shall, as the Mandatory Power withdraws its armed forces, be progressively turned over to the Commission, which shall act in conformity with the recommendations of the General Assembly, under the guidance of the Security Council. The Mandatory Power shall to the fullest possible extent coordinate its plans for withdrawal with the plans of the Commission to take over and administer areas which have been evacuated.

In the discharge of this administrative responsibility the Commission shall have authority to issue necessary regulations and take other measures as required.

The Mandatory Power shall not take any action to prevent, obstruct or delay the implementation by the Commission of the measures recommended by the General Assembly.

3. On its arrival in Palestine the Commission shall proceed to carry out measures for the establishment of the frontiers of the Arab and Jewish States and the City of Jerusalem in accordance with the general lines of the recommendations of the General Assembly on the partition of Palestine. Nevertheless, the boundaries as described in Part II of this Plan are to be modified in such a way that village areas as a rule will not be divided by state boundaries unless pressing reasons make that necessary.

4. The Commission, after consultation with the democratic parties and other public organizations of the Arab and Jewish States, shall select

and establish in each State as rapidly as possible a Provisional Council of Government. The activities of both the Arab and Jewish Provisional Councils of Government shall be carried out under the general direction of the Commission.

If by 1 April 1948 a Provisional Council of Government cannot be selected for either of the States, or, if selected, cannot carry out its functions, the Commission shall communicate that fact to the Security Council for such action with respect to that State as the Security Council may deem proper, and to the Secretary-General for communication to the Members of the United Nations.

5. Subject to the provisions of these recommendations, during the transitional period the Provisional Councils of Government, acting under the Commission, shall have full authority in the areas under their control, including authority over matters of immigration and land regulation. . . .

PART III, CITY OF JERUSALEM

A. The City of Jerusalem shall be established as a corpus separatum under a Special International Regime and shall be administered by the United Nations. The Trusteeship Council shall be designated to discharge the responsibilities of the Administering Authority on behalf of the United Nations.

DOCUMENT NO. 16

UNITED NATIONS RESOLUTION ON THE DISPOSITION OF PALESTINE, 1947[16]

General Assembly Resolution 181 essentially accepted the majority recommendations (described in Document No. 15) of the United Nations Special Committee on Palestine (UNSCOP), which sought a partition of Palestine and placing Jerusalem under special international status. Here, as with the UNSCOP report, the detailed descriptions of the boundaries have been omitted.

γ   γ   γ

16. *Yearbook of the United Nations, 1947–48* (Lake Success, NY: United Nations Office of Public Information, 1949), 247–257.

Excerpts of United Nations General Assembly Resolution 181
Plan of Partition for Palestine

November 29, 1947

The General Assembly, Having met in special session at the request of the mandatory Power to constitute and instruct a Special Committee to prepare for the consideration of the question of the future Government of Palestine at the second regular session;

Having constituted a Special Committee and instructed it to investigate all questions and issues relevant to the problem of Palestine, and to prepare proposals for the solution of the problem, and

Having received and examined the report of the Special Committee (document A/364)(1) including a number of unanimous recommendations and a plan of partition with economic union approved by the majority of the Special Committee,

Considers that the present situation in Palestine is one which is likely to impair the general welfare and friendly relations among nations;

Takes note of the declaration by the mandatory Power that it plans to complete its evacuation of Palestine by 1 August 1948;

Recommends to the United Kingdom, as the mandatory Power for Palestine, and to all other Members of the United Nations the adoption and implementation, with regard to the future Government of Palestine, of the Plan of Partition with Economic Union set out below;

Requests that

The Security Council take the necessary measures as provided for in the plan for its implementation;

The Security Council consider, if circumstances during the transitional period require such consideration, whether the situation in Palestine constitutes a threat to the peace. If it decides that such a threat exists, and in order to maintain international peace and security, the Security Council should supplement the authorization of the General Assembly by taking measures, under Articles 39 and 41 of the Charter, to empower the United Nations Commission, as provided in this resolution, to exercise in Palestine the functions which are assigned to it by this resolution;

The Security Council determine as a threat to the peace, breach of the peace or act of aggression, in accordance with Article 39 of the Charter, any attempt to alter by force the settlement envisaged by this resolution;

The Trusteeship Council be informed of the responsibilities envisaged for it in this plan;

Calls upon the inhabitants of Palestine to take such steps as may be necessary on their part to put this plan into effect;

Appeals to all Governments and all peoples to refrain from taking any action which might hamper or delay the carrying out of these recommendations, and

Authorizes the Secretary-General to reimburse travel and subsistence expenses of the members of the Commission referred to in Part 1, Section B, Paragraph I below, on such basis and in such form as he may determine most appropriate in the circumstances, and to provide the Commission with the necessary staff to assist in carrying out the functions assigned to the Commission by the General Assembly.

The General Assembly,

Authorizes the Secretary-General to draw from the Working Capital Fund a sum not to exceed 2,000,000 dollars for the purposes set forth in the last paragraph of the resolution on the future government of Palestine.

PLAN OF PARTITION WITH ECONOMIC UNION

PART I

Future constitution and government of Palestine

A. TERMINATION OF MANDATE, PARTITION AND INDE-PENDENCE

1.   The Mandate for Palestine shall terminate as soon as possible but in any case not later than 1 August 1948.

2.   The armed forces of the mandatory Power shall be progressively withdrawn from Palestine, the withdrawal to be completed as soon as possible but in any case not later than 1 August 1948.

The mandatory Power shall advise the Commission, as far in advance as possible, of its intention to terminate the Mandate and to evacuate each area.

The mandatory Power shall use its best endeavors to ensure than an area situated in the territory of the Jewish State, including a seaport and hinterland adequate to provide facilities for a substantial immigration, shall be evacuated at the earliest possible date and in any event not later than 1 February 1948.

3.   Independent Arab and Jewish States and the Special International Regime for the City of Jerusalem, set forth in part III of this plan, shall come into existence in Palestine two months after the evacuation of the armed forces of the mandatory Power has been completed but in any case not later than 1 October 1948. The boundaries of the Arab State, the Jewish State, and the City of Jerusalem shall be as described in parts II and III below.

4.   The period between the adoption by the General Assembly of its recommendation on the question of Palestine and the establishment of the independence of the Arab and Jewish States shall be a transitional period.

B. STEPS PREPARATORY TO INDEPENDENCE

1.   A Commission shall be set up consisting of one representative of each of five Member States. The Members represented on the Commis-

sion shall be elected by the General Assembly on as broad a basis, geographically and otherwise, as possible.

2.   The administration of Palestine shall, as the mandatory Power withdraws its armed forces, be progressively turned over to the Commission; which shall act in conformity with the recommendations of the General Assembly, under the guidance of the Security Council. The mandatory Power shall to the fullest possible extent coordinate its plans for withdrawal with the plans of the Commission to take over and administer areas which have been evacuated.

In the discharge of this administrative responsibility the Commission shall have authority to issue necessary regulations and take other measures as required.

The mandatory Power shall not take any action to prevent, obstruct or delay the implementation by the Commission of the measures recommended by the General Assembly.

3.   On its arrival in Palestine the Commission shall proceed to carry out measures for the establishment of the frontiers of the Arab and Jewish States and the City of Jerusalem in accordance with the general lines of the recommendations of the General Assembly on the partition of Palestine. Nevertheless, the boundaries as described in part II of this plan are to be modified in such a way that village areas as a rule will not be divided by state boundaries unless pressing reasons make that necessary.

4.   The Commission, after consultation with the democratic parties and other public organizations of The Arab and Jewish States, shall select and establish in each State as rapidly as possible a Provisional Council of Government. The activities of both the Arab and Jewish Provisional Councils of Government shall be carried out under the general direction of the Commission. . . .

Adopted at the 128th plenary meeting:

In favor: 33
Australia, Belgium, Bolivia, Brazil, Byelorussian S.S.R., Canada, Costa

Rica, Czechoslovakia, Denmark, Dominican Republic, Ecuador, France, Guatemala, Haiti, Iceland, Liberia, Luxembourg, Netherlands, New Zealand, Nicaragua, Norway, Panama, Paraguay, Peru, Philippines, Poland, Sweden, Ukrainian S.S.R., Union of South Africa, U.S.A., U.S.S.R., Uruguay, Venezuela.

Against: 13

Afghanistan, Cuba, Egypt, Greece, India, Iran, Iraq, Lebanon, Pakistan, Saudi Arabia, Syria, Turkey, Yemen.

Abstained: 10

Argentina, Chile, China, Colombia, El Salvador, Ethiopia, Honduras, Mexico, United Kingdom, Yugoslavia. . . .

DOCUMENT NO. 17

UN SECURITY COUNCIL RESOLUTION 242 ON PEACE IN THE MIDDLE EAST[17]

The Security Council passed Resolution 242 in the aftermath of the 1967 "Six Day War" in which Israel captured portions of Jordan, Egypt, and Syria. This resolution became the basis of land for peace initiatives leading to the Camp David Accords of 1979, the Madrid peace initiative of 1991, the Oslo Accords of 1993, and Camp David II and at Sharm al-Sheik in 2000–2001. Sponsored by the United Kingdom and France, the Resolution has been accepted by Egypt, Jordan, Lebanon, Israel, and the PLO.

γ   γ   γ

UN Resolution 242
The Situation in the Middle East

November 22, 1967

The Security Council,
Expressing its continuing concern with the grave situation in the Middle East.

17. *Yearbook of the United Nations, 1967* (New York: United Nations Office of Public Information, 1969), 257–258.

Emphasizing the inadmissibility of the acquisition of territory by war and the need to work for a just and lasting peace in which every state in the area can live in security.

Emphasizing further that all member states in their acceptance of the Charter of the United Nations have undertaken a commitment to act in accordance with Article 2 of the Charter.

1. Affirms that the fulfillment of Charter principles requires the establishment of a just and lasting peace in the Middle East which should include the application of both the following principles:

   1. Withdrawal of Israeli armed forces from territories of recent conflict.

   2. Termination of all claims or states of belligerency and respect for and acknowledgment of the sovereignty, territorial integrity and political independence of every state in the area and their right to live in peace within secure and recognized boundaries free from threats or acts of force.

2. Affirms further the necessity for:

   1. Guaranteeing freedom of navigation through international waterways in the area.

   2. Achieving a just settlement of the refugee problem.

   3. Guaranteeing the territorial inviolability and political independence of every state in the area through measures including the establishment of demilitarized zones.

3. Requests the Secretary General to designate a special representative to proceed to the Middle East to establish and maintain contacts within the state concerned in order to promote agreement and assist efforts to achieve a peaceful and accepted settlement in accordance with the provisions and principles in this resolution.

DOCUMENT NO. 18

UN GENERAL ASSEMBLY RESOLUTION EQUATING ZIONISM WITH RACISM[18]

In the wake of the June 1967 war, the membership of the General Assembly grew increasingly critical of Israel, passing this controversial 1975 Resolution equating Zionism with racism and with Apartheid regimes such as Rhodesia and South Africa. The General Assembly revoked the Resolution in December 1991, only the second time it has done so.

γ   γ   γ

General Assembly Resolution 3379

November 10, 1975

RECALLING its resolution 1904 (XVIII) of 20 November 1963, proclaiming the United Nations Declaration on the Elimination of All Forms of Racial Discrimination, and in particular its affirmation that "any doctrine of racial differentiation or superiority is scientifically false, morally condemnable, socially unjust and dangerous" and its expression of alarm at "the manifestations of racial discrimination still in evidence in some areas in the world, some of which are imposed by certain Governments by means of legislative, administrative or other measures",

RECALLING ALSO that, in its resolution 3151 G (XXVIII) of 14 December 1953, the General Assembly condemned, inter alia, the unholy alliance between South African racism and Zionism,

TAKING NOTE of the Declaration of Mexico on the Equality of Women and Their Contribution to Development and Peace 1975, proclaimed by the World Conference of the International Women's Year, held at Mexico City from 19 June to 2 July 1975, which promulgated the principle that "international cooperation and peace require the achievement of national liberation and independence, the elimination of colonialism and neocolonialism, foreign occupation, Zionism, apartheid

18. *Yearbook of the United Nations, 1975, vol. 29* (New York: United Nations Office of Public Information, 1978), 599–600.

and racial discrimination in all its forms, as well as the recognition of the dignity of peoples and their right to self-determination",

TAKING NOTE ALSO of resolution 77 (XII) adopted by the Assembly of Heads of State and Government of the Organization of African Unity at its twelfth ordinary session, held at Kampala from 28 July to 1 August 1975, which considered "that the racist regime in occupied Palestine and the racist regime in Zimbabwe and South Africa have a common imperialist origin, forming a whole and having the same racist structure and being organically linked in their policy aimed at repression of the dignity and integrity of the human being",

TAKING NOTE ALSO of the Political Declaration and Strategy to Strengthen International Peace and Security and to Intensify Solidarity and Mutual Assistance among Non-Aligned Countries, adopted at the Conference of Ministers for Foreign Affairs of Non-Aligned Countries held at Lima from 25 to 30 August 1975, which most severely condemned Zionism as a threat to world peace and security and called upon all countries to oppose this racist and imperialist ideology,

DETERMINES that Zionism is a form of racism and racial discrimination.

DOCUMENT NO. 19

THE UN DISPATCHES PEACEKEEPERS TO THE MIDDLE EAST, 1956[19]

Egyptian leader Abdel Gamel Nasser nationalized the Suez Canal on July 26, 1956. In response, the British, French, and Israeli governments colluded in secret to invade Egypt and overthrow Nasser, an attack launched on October 29. The United Nations General Assembly held an emergency session where, under the Uniting for Peace Resolution, it passed Resolution 997, supported by both Washington and Moscow, pressuring Britain and France into a cease-fire. The General Assembly also authorized a large multinational peacekeeping operation of 6,000 troops.

19. *Yearbook of the United Nations, 1956* (New York: United Nations Office of Public Information, 1957), 35.

γ   γ   γ

United Nations General Assembly Resolution 997
The Suez Crisis

November 2, 1956

The United States submitted the draft for the following Resolution, which was passed by the General Assembly on 2 November 1956, with 64 votes for, 5 against, and 6 abstentions:

The General Assembly,

Noting the disregard on many occasions by parties to the Israel–Arab armistice agreements of 1949 of the terms of such agreements, and that the armed forces of Israel have penetrated deeply into Egyptian territory in violation of the General Armistice Agreement between Egypt and Israel of 24 February 1949,

Noting that armed forces of France and the United Kingdom of Great Britain and Northern Ireland are conducting military operations against Egyptian territory,

Noting that traffic through the Suez Canal is now interrupted to the serious prejudice of many nations,

Expressing its grave concern over these developments,

1. Urges as a matter of priority that all parties now involved in hostilities in the area agree to an immediate cease-fire and, as part thereof, halt the movement of military forces and arms into the area;

2. Urges the parties to the armistice agreements promptly to withdraw all forces behind the armistice lines, to desist from raids across the armistice lines into neighboring territory, and to observe scrupulously the provisions of all the armistice agreements;

3. Recommends that all Member States refrain from introducing military goods in the area of hostilities and in general refrain from any acts which would delay or prevent the implementation of the present Resolution;

4. Urges that, upon the cease-fire being effective, steps be taken to re-open the Suez Canal and restore secure freedom of navigation;

5. Requests the Secretary-General to observe and report promptly on the compliance with the present Resolution to the Security Council and to the General Assembly, for such further action as they may deem appropriate in accordance with the Charter;

6. Decides to remain in emergency session pending compliance with the present Resolution.

DOCUMENT NO. 20

UN RESOLUTION ADDRESSING IRAQ'S INVASION OF KUWAIT, 1990[20]

In the aftermath of the Iraqi invasion of Kuwait in August 1990, the Security Council became a forum for 29 resolutions against Iraq, the most significant—SCR 660 and SCR 678—(see Document 21) authorizing the possibility of the use of force, the first time the Security Council had approved such a measure since the Korean War. Security Council Resolution 660 was the first of a series of UN actions dealing with Iraq's invasion of Kuwait. It laid the groundwork for subsequent action and put Iraq on notice that its invasion was deemed unacceptable by the international community.

γ   γ   γ

United Nations Security Council Resolution 660

August 2, 1990

The Security Council,

Alarmed by the invasion of Kuwait on 2 August 1990 by the military forces of Iraq,

Determining that there exists a breach of international peace and security as regards the Iraqi invasion of Kuwait,

20. *Yearbook of the United Nations, 1990, vol. 44* (New York: United Nations Office of Public Information, 1999), 190.

Acting under Articles 39 and 40 of the Charter of the United Nations,

1. Condemns the Iraqi invasion of Kuwait;

2. Demands that Iraq withdraw immediately and unconditionally all its forces to the positions in which they were located on 1 August 1990;

3. Calls upon Iraq and Kuwait to begin immediately intensive negotiations for the resolution of their differences and supports all efforts in this regard, and especially those of the League of Arab States;

4. Decides to meet again as necessary to consider further steps with to ensure compliance with the present resolution.

DOCUMENT NO. 21

UN RESOLUTION ON THE POSSIBLE USE OF FORCE AGAINST IRAQ[21]

Giving Iraq another chance to comply with Security Council Resolution 660 (see Document No. 20), Resolution 678 also raised the possibility of the use of force against Iraq under Chapter VII of the United Nations Charter, the first time the Security Council had considered such a measure since the Korean War.

γ γ γ

Security Council Resolution 678

November 29, 1990

Adopted by the Security Council at its 2963rd meeting on 29 November 1990

The Security Council,

Recalling, and reaffirming its resolutions 660 (1990) of 2 August (1990), 661 (1990) of 6 August 1990, 662 (1990) of 9 August 1990, 664 (1990) of 18 August 1990, 665 (1990) of 25 August 1990, 666 (1990) of 13 September 1990, 667 (1990) of 16 September 1990, 669 (1990) of 24 Sep-

---

21. *Yearbook of the United Nations, 1990* (New York: United Nations Office of Public Information, 1999), 204.

tember 1990, 670 (1990) of 25 September 1990, 674 (1990) of of 29 October 1990 and 677 (1990) of 28 November 1990.

Noting that, despite all efforts by the United Nations, Iraq refuses to comply with its obligation to implement resolution 660 (1990) and the above-mentioned subsequent relevant resolutions, in flagrant contempt of the Security Council,

Mindful of its duties and responsibilities under the Charter of the United Nations for the maintenance and preservation of international peace and security,

Determined to secure full compliance with its decisions,

Acting under Chapter VII of the Charter,

1. Demands that Iraq comply fully with resolution 660 (1990) and all subsequent relevant resolutions, and decides, while maintaining all its decisions, to allow Iraq one final opportunity, as a pause of goodwill, to do so;

2. Authorizes Member States cooperating with the Government of Kuwait, unless Iraq on or before 15 January 1991 fully implements, as set forth in paragraph 1 above, the foregoing resolutions, to use all necessary means to uphold and implement resolution 660 (1990) and all subsequent relevant resolutions and to restore international peace and security in the area;

3. Requests all States to provide appropriate support for the actions undertaken in pursuance of paragraph 2 of the present resolution;

4. Requests the States concerned to keep the Security Council regularly informed on the progress of actions undertaken pursuant to paragraphs 2 and 3 of the present resolution;

5. Decides to remain seized of the matter.

DOCUMENT NO. 22

UN RESOLUTION ON WEAPONS INSPECTIONS IN IRAQ, 2002[22]

Washington gave as a pretext for its 2003 war against Iraq (among a multiplicity of rationales) the alleged Iraqi development of weapons of mass destruction. Security Council Resolution 1441 was pushed by the British

22. The full text of United Nations Security Council Resolution 1441 is obtainable at the United Nations website: http://www.un.org/Docs/scres/2002/sc2002.htm

and Americans in the hope of securing UN support for an invasion, but its precise meaning and aims provoked great controversy among the permanent members of the Security Council.

γ   γ   γ

Text of UN Security Council Resolution 1441 on Iraq

November 8, 2002

United Kingdom of Great Britain and Northern Ireland and United States of America

Adopted as Resolution 1441 at Security Council meeting 4644, 8 November 2002

The Security Council,

Recalling all its previous relevant resolutions, in particular its resolutions 661 (1990) of 6 August 1990, 678 (1990) of 29 November 1990, 686 (1991) of 2 March 1991, 687 (1991) of 3 April 1991, 688 (1991) of 5 April 1991, 707 (1991) of 15 August 1991, 715 (1991) of 11 October 1991, 986 (1995) of 14 April 1995, and 1284 (1999) of 17 December 1999, and all the relevant statements of its President,

Recalling also its resolution 1382 (2001) of 29 November 2001 and its intention to implement it fully,

Recognizing the threat Iraq's noncompliance with Council resolutions and proliferation of weapons of mass destruction and long-range missiles poses to international peace and security,

Recalling that its resolution 678 (1990) authorized Member States to use all necessary means to uphold and implement its resolution 660 (1990) of 2 August 1990 and all relevant resolutions subsequent to resolution 660 (1990) and to restore international peace and security in the area,

Further recalling that its resolution 687 (1991) imposed obligations on Iraq as a necessary step for achievement of its stated objective of restoring international peace and security in the area,

Deploring the fact that Iraq has not provided an accurate, full, final, and complete disclosure, as required by resolution 687 (1991), of all aspects of its programs to develop weapons of mass destruction and ballistic missiles with a range greater than one hundred and fifty kilometers, and of all holdings of such weapons, their components and production facilities and locations, as well as all other nuclear programs, including any which it claims are for purposes not related to nuclear-weapons-usable material,

Deploring further that Iraq repeatedly obstructed immediate, unconditional, and unrestricted access to sites designated by the United Nations Special Commission (UNSCOM) and the International Atomic Energy Agency (IAEA), failed to cooperate fully and unconditionally with UNSCOM and IAEA weapons inspectors, as required by resolution 687 (1991), and ultimately ceased all cooperation with UNSCOM and the IAEA in 1998,

Deploring the absence, since December 1998, in Iraq of international monitoring, inspection, and verification, as required by relevant resolutions, of weapons of mass destruction and ballistic missiles, in spite of the Council's repeated demands that Iraq provide immediate, unconditional, and unrestricted access to the United Nations Monitoring, Verification and Inspection Commission (UNMOVIC), established in resolution 1284 (1999) as the successor organization to UNSCOM, and the IAEA, and regretting the consequent prolonging of the crisis in the region and the suffering of the Iraqi people,

Deploring also that the Government of Iraq has failed to comply with its commitments pursuant to resolution 687 (1991) with regard to terrorism, pursuant to resolution 688 (1991) to end repression of its civilian population and to provide access by international humanitarian organizations to all those in need of assistance in Iraq, and pursuant to resolutions 686 (1991), 687 (1991), and 1284 (1999) to return or cooperate in accounting for Kuwaiti and third country nationals wrongfully detained by Iraq, or to return Kuwaiti property wrongfully seized by Iraq,

Recalling that in its resolution 687 (1991) the Council declared that a ceasefire would be based on acceptance by Iraq of the provisions of that resolution, including the obligations on Iraq contained therein,

Determined to ensure full and immediate compliance by Iraq without conditions or restrictions with its obligations under resolution 687 (1991) and other relevant resolutions and recalling that the resolutions of the Council constitute the governing standard of Iraqi compliance,

Recalling that the effective operation of UNMOVIC, as the successor organization to the Special Commission, and the IAEA is essential for the implementation of resolution 687 (1991) and other relevant resolutions,

Noting the letter dated 16 September 2002 from the Minister for Foreign Affairs of Iraq addressed to the Secretary-General is a necessary first step toward rectifying Iraq's continued failure to comply with relevant Council resolutions,

Noting further the letter dated 8 October 2002 from the Executive Chairman of UNMOVIC and the Director-General of the IAEA to General Al-Saadi of the Government of Iraq laying out the practical arrangements, as a follow-up to their meeting in Vienna, that are prerequisites for the resumption of inspections in Iraq by UNMOVIC and the IAEA, and expressing the gravest concern at the continued failure by the Government of Iraq to provide confirmation of the arrangements as laid out in that letter,

Reaffirming the commitment of all Member States to the sovereignty and territorial integrity of Iraq, Kuwait, and the neighboring States,

Commending the Secretary-General and members of the League of Arab States and its Secretary-General for their efforts in this regard,

Determined to secure full compliance with its decisions,

Acting under Chapter VII of the Charter of the United Nations,

1. Decides that Iraq has been and remains in material breach of its obligations under relevant resolutions, including resolution 687 (1991), in particular through Iraq's failure to cooperate with United Nations inspectors and the IAEA, and to complete the actions required under paragraphs 8 to 13 of resolution 687 (1991);

2. Decides, while acknowledging paragraph 1 above, to afford Iraq, by this resolution, a final opportunity to comply with its disarmament obligations under relevant resolutions of the Council; and accordingly decides to set up an enhanced inspection regime with the aim of bringing to full and verified completion the disarmament process established by resolution 687 (1991) and subsequent resolutions of the Council;

3. Decides that, in order to begin to comply with its disarmament obligations, in addition to submitting the required biannual declarations, the Government of Iraq shall provide to UNMOVIC, the IAEA, and the Council, not later than 30 days from the date of this resolution, a currently accurate, full, and complete declaration of all aspects of its programs to develop chemical, biological, and nuclear weapons, ballistic missiles, and other delivery systems such as unmanned aerial vehicles and dispersal systems designed for use on aircraft, including any holdings and precise locations of such weapons, components, sub-components, stocks of agents, and related material and equipment, the locations and work of its research, development and production facilities, as well as all other chemical, biological, and nuclear programs, including any which it claims are for purposes not related to weapon production or material;

4. Decides that false statements or omissions in the declarations submitted by Iraq pursuant to this resolution and failure by Iraq at any time to comply with, and cooperate fully in the implementation of, this resolution shall constitute a further material breach of Iraq's obligations and will be reported to the Council for assessment in accordance with paragraphs 11 and 12 below;

5. Decides that Iraq shall provide UNMOVIC and the IAEA immediate, unimpeded, unconditional, and unrestricted access to any and all, including underground, areas, facilities, buildings, equipment, records, and means of transport which they wish to inspect, as well as immediate, unimpeded, unrestricted, and private access to all officials and other persons whom UNMOVIC or the IAEA wish to interview in the mode or location of UNMOVIC's or the IAEA's choice pursuant to any aspect of their mandates; further decides that UNMOVIC and the IAEA may at their discretion conduct interviews inside or outside of Iraq, may facilitate the travel of those interviewed and family members

outside of Iraq, and that, at the sole discretion of UNMOVIC and the IAEA, such interviews may occur without the presence of observers from the Iraqi Government; and instructs UNMOVIC and requests the IAEA to resume inspections no later than 45 days following adoption of this resolution and to update the Council 60 days thereafter;

6. Endorses the 8 October 2002 letter from the Executive Chairman of UNMOVIC and the Director-General of the IAEA to General Al-Saadi of the Government of Iraq, which is annexed hereto, and decides that the contents of the letter shall be binding upon Iraq;

7. Decides further that, in view of the prolonged interruption by Iraq of the presence of UNMOVIC and the IAEA and in order for them to accomplish the tasks set forth in this resolution and all previous relevant resolutions and notwithstanding prior understandings, the Council hereby establishes the following revised or additional authorities, which shall be binding upon Iraq, to facilitate their work in Iraq:

—UNMOVIC and the IAEA shall determine the composition of their inspection teams and ensure that these teams are composed of the most qualified and experienced experts available;

—All UNMOVIC and IAEA personnel shall enjoy the privileges and immunities, corresponding to those of experts on mission, provided in the Convention on Privileges and Immunities of the United Nations and the Agreement on the Privileges and Immunities of the IAEA;

—UNMOVIC and the IAEA shall have unrestricted rights of entry into and out of Iraq, the right to free, unrestricted, and immediate movement to and from inspection sites, and the right to inspect any sites and buildings, including immediate, unimpeded, unconditional, and unrestricted access to Presidential Sites equal to that at other sites, notwithstanding the provisions of resolution 1154 (1998);

—UNMOVIC and the IAEA shall have the right to be provided by Iraq the names of all personnel currently and formerly associated with Iraq's chemical, biological, nuclear, and ballistic missile programs and the associated research, development, and production facilities;

—Security of UNMOVIC and IAEA facilities shall be ensured by sufficient United Nations security guards;

—UNMOVIC and the IAEA shall have the right to declare, for the purposes of freezing a site to be inspected, exclusion zones, including surrounding areas and transit corridors, in which Iraq will suspend ground and aerial movement so that nothing is changed in or taken out of a site being inspected;

—UNMOVIC and the IAEA shall have the free and unrestricted use and landing of fixed- and rotary-winged aircraft, including manned and unmanned reconnaissance vehicles;

—UNMOVIC and the IAEA shall have the right at their sole discretion verifiably to remove, destroy, or render harmless all prohibited weapons, subsystems, components, records, materials, and other related items, and the right to impound or close any facilities or equipment for the production thereof; and

—UNMOVIC and the IAEA shall have the right to free import and use of equipment or materials for inspections and to seize and export any equipment, materials, or documents taken during inspections, without search of UNMOVIC or IAEA personnel or official or personal baggage;

8. Decides further that Iraq shall not take or threaten hostile acts directed against any representative or personnel of the United Nations or the IAEA or of any Member State taking action to uphold any Council resolution;

9. Requests the Secretary-General immediately to notify Iraq of this resolution, which is binding on Iraq; demands that Iraq confirm within seven days of that notification its intention to comply fully with this resolution; and demands further that Iraq cooperate immediately, unconditionally, and actively with UNMOVIC and the IAEA;

10. Requests all Member States to give full support to UNMOVIC and the IAEA in the discharge of their mandates, including by providing any information related to prohibited programs or other aspects of their mandates, including on Iraqi attempts since 1998 to acquire prohibited items, and by recommending sites to be inspected, persons to be interviewed, conditions of such interviews, and data to be collected, the re-

sults of which shall be reported to the Council by UNMOVIC and the IAEA;

11. Directs the Executive Chairman of UNMOVIC and the Director-General of the IAEA to report immediately to the Council any interference by Iraq with inspection activities, as well as any failure by Iraq to comply with its disarmament obligations, including its obligations regarding inspections under this resolution;

12. Decides to convene immediately upon receipt of a report in accordance with paragraphs 4 or 11 above, in order to consider the situation and the need for full compliance with all of the relevant Council resolutions in order to secure international peace and security;

13. Recalls, in that context, that the Council has repeatedly warned Iraq that it will face serious consequences as a result of its continued violations of its obligations;

14. Decides to remain seized of the matter.

DOCUMENT NO. 23

THE SECRETARY GENERAL'S REPORT ON PEACEKEEPING FAILURES[23]

This is a portion of a larger report by the Secretary General featuring selected case studies summarizing the lessons learned. These excerpts focus on the UN and the crisis in Somalia. Offered here are frank self-appraisals, identifying mistakes made and suggesting how success might be achieved in the future.

γ   γ   γ

Report of the Secretary-General
The causes of conflict and the promotion of durable peace and sustainable development in Africa

---

23. A full copy of the report can be obtained at the UN's official website at: http://www.un.org/ecosocdev/geninfo/afrec/sgreport/report.htm

Lessons learned:

31. The international community's perception of peacekeeping has been greatly shaped by the United Nations experience in Somalia. The memories of that operation continue to hobble the United Nations capacity to respond swiftly and decisively to crises. While the civilian population in Somalia derived significant benefits from the United Nations involvement, including the end of starvation, the United Nations Operation in Somalia was also the first United Nations operation to be withdrawn by the Security Council before completing its mission. The Security Council based that decision on the fact that, despite the operation's humanitarian accomplishments, no political progress had been made because of lack of commitment on the part of key Somali factions not interested in a settlement.

32. The consequences of the retreat from Somalia and the reluctance to again commit international resources and political capital soon became evident as the international community agonized over how to respond to the tragedy that began to unfold in Rwanda. Hundreds of thousands of lives were lost in the course of the genocide that was perpetrated in full view of the international community. That experience highlighted the crucial importance of swift intervention in a conflict and, above all, of political will to act in the face of a catastrophe. The horrifying suffering of the Rwandan people sends the clear and unmistakable message that the international community must never again tolerate such inaction.

33. A positive lesson was drawn from the United Nations Operation in Mozambique. There, the United Nations influence was augmented through constant dialogue with the parties on the ground and with other States. The operation, became a conduit for international resources, and a binding element for international action, a focal point, a symbol and a catalyst for efforts for peace. The United Nations experience in Mozambique showed that, in the right circumstances, peacekeeping operations can offer a flexible and uniquely adapted means to confront conflict in Africa. Its success testifies to the contribution that the United Nations can make as an impartial and legitimate actor for peace. It also indicates the Organization's potential to strengthen and direct interna-

tional engagement within a conflict that might otherwise be exacerbated by negligence or by manipulation from outside, and the extent to which unanimity of purpose and willingness to act in a coherent manner can enhance the authority of the international community.

34. The successive United Nations deployments in Angola have shown the vital role that can be played by a United Nations operation in sustaining a peace process in even the most adverse circumstances, but they have also indicated the crucial need for realistic peace agreements, and the importance of having a credible deterrent capacity within a peacekeeping operation in situations that remain dangerous and volatile. The ongoing risk of conflict has demonstrated, further, how access to resources by warring parties can foster violence, and has highlighted the impact that international business interests can have on the success or failure of peace efforts.

DOCUMENT NO. 24

THE SECRETARY GENERAL ACCEPTS UN RESPONSIBILITY FOR THE MASSACRES IN RWANDA[24]

In Rwanda, one of the UN's greatest failures to date, the international community witnessed the massacre of an estimated 800,000 people, shattering the UN's credibility in the process. Five years later, Secretary General Kofi Annan appointed an Independent Inquiry to investigate why the genocide in Rwanda was allowed to happen.

γ   γ   γ

Statement on Receiving the Report of the Independent Inquiry into the Actions of the United Nations During the 1994 Genocide in Rwanda
December 16, 1999

The United Nations was founded at the end of a war during which genocide had been committed on a horrific scale. Its prime objective was to prevent such a conflict from ever happening again. Three years

24. http://www.fas.org/man/dod-101/ops/war/docs/sgsm_rwanda.htm

later, the General Assembly adopted a Convention under which States accepted an obligation to "prevent and punish" this most heinous of crimes.

In 1994 the whole international community—the United Nations and its Members States—failed to honor that obligation. Approximately 800,000 Rwandans were slaughtered by their fellow countrymen and women, for no other reason than that they belonged to a particular ethnic group. That is genocide in its purest and most evil form.

All of us must bitterly regret that we did not do more to prevent it. There was a United Nations force in the country at the time, but it was neither mandated nor equipped for the kind of forceful action which would have been needed to prevent or halt the genocide. On behalf of the United Nations, I [Secretary General Annan] acknowledge this failure and express my deep remorse.

In view of the enormity of what happened, and the questions that continued, five years after the event, to surround the actions of the United Nations before and during the crisis, in March this year I commissioned a completely independent Inquiry into those actions, with the approval of the Security Council.

The Inquiry enjoyed full and unrestricted access to United Nations records, including internal documents and cables. It has now completed its work, and its findings have been made public. I thank Mr. Carlsson, Professor Han and General Kupolati for their Report, which is thorough and objective. I fully accept their conclusions, including those which reflect on officials of the UN Secretariat, of whom I myself was one. I also welcome the emphasis which the Inquiry has put on the lessons to be learnt from this tragedy, and the careful and well argued recommendations it has made with the aim of ensuring that the United Nations can and will act to prevent or halt any other such catastrophe in the future.

These recommendations merit very serious attention, leading to prompt and effective action—by the Secretariat, by the Security Council, and by the international community as a whole.

As the Report itself acknowledges, some steps have already been taken over the past few years to improve the capacity of the United Nations to respond to conflicts, and specifically to respond to some of the mistakes made in Rwanda. But much remains to be done. It was precisely in the hope of preventing further such tragedies that, in my address to the General Assembly in September, I called on the international community to reflect on ways in which the United Nations could intervene more promptly, and more effectively, to prevent or halt massive and systematic violations of human rights.

More broadly, in my own Report on the equally shameful events which occurred at Srebrenica only a year after those in Rwanda, I urged Member States to engage in a process of reflection and analysis, aimed at improving the capacity of the United Nations to respond to various forms of conflict. I intend very soon to make further recommendations on the form which this process should take.

Both Reports—my own on Srebrenica, and that of the independent Inquiry on Rwanda—reflect a profound determination to present the truth about these calamities. Of all my aims as Secretary-General, there is none to which I feel more deeply committed than that of enabling the United Nations never again to fail in protecting a civilian population from genocide or mass slaughter.

DOCUMENT NO. 25

THE UN'S RANKING OF THE MOST AND LEAST LIVABLE COUNTRIES[25]

The United Nation's Human Development Index (HDI) ranks nations according to their inhabitants' quality of life rather than strictly by more traditional economic indicators. The criteria include life expectancy, educational attainment, and adjusted real income.

γ   γ   γ

25. *Human Development Report 2003. Millennium Development Goals: A Compact Among Nations to End Human Poverty* (New York: Oxford University Press, 2003), 237–240.

UN Human Development Index, 2003

"Least Livable" Countries, 2003

1.	Sierra Leone	14.	Malawi
2.	Niger	15.	Côte d'Ivoire
3.	Burkina Faso	16.	Tanzania
4.	Mali	17.	Benin
5.	Burundi	18.	Rwanda
6.	Mozambique	19.	Guinea
7.	Ethiopia	20.	Senegal
8.	Central African Rep.	21.	Eritrea
9.	Dem. Rep. of Congo	22.	Mauritania
10.	Guinea-Bissau	23.	Djibouti
11.	Chad	24.	Nigeria
12.	Angola	25.	Gambia
13.	Zambia		

"Most Livable" Countries, 2003

1.	Norway	14.	Finland
2.	Iceland	15.	Luxembourg
3.	Sweden	16.	Austria
4.	Australia	17.	France
5.	Netherlands	18.	Germany
6.	Belgium	19.	Spain
7.	United States	20.	New Zealand
8.	Canada	21.	Italy
9.	Japan	22.	Israel
10.	Switzerland	23.	Portugal
11.	Denmark	24.	Greece
12.	Ireland	25.	Cyprus
13.	United Kingdom		

DOCUMENT NO. 26

THE USE OF THE UN SECURITY COUNCIL VETO[26]

Only a handful of vetoes have been cast with vital international interests at stake, while 59 have been used to block the admission of states. The United States did not cast its first veto until 1970, but has issued 79 since then. The first veto exercised by the People's Republic of China was not until 25 August 1972. Between 1946 and 1971, the Chinese seat on the Security Council was occupied by the Taiwan-based Republic of China, which used the veto only once (to block Mongolia's application for membership in 1955).

γ   γ   γ

Table shows number of times veto was cast, by country

Period	China	France	Britain	U.S.	USSR/Russia	Total
2004	–	–	–	1	1	2
2003	–	–	–	2	–	2
2002	–	–	–	2	–	2
2001	–	–	–	2	–	2
2000	–	–	–	–	–	0
1999	1	–	–	–	–	1
1998	–	–	–	–	–	0
1997	1	–	–	2	–	3
1996	–	–	–	–	–	0
1986–95	–	3	8	24	2	37
1976–85	–	9	11	34	6	60
1966–75	2	2	10	12	57	33
1956–65	–	2	3	–	26	31
1946–55	1	2	–	–	80	83
Total:	4–5	18	32	79	122	256

26. From the Global Policy Forum website at: www.globalpolicy.org/security/data/ vetotab.htm See also Sydney d. Bailey and Sam Dawes, *The Procedure of the UN Security Council.* Third Edition (New York: Oxford University Press, 1998), 231–239 [Table compiled by Global Policy Forum and Giji Gya from UN information].

DOCUMENT NO. 27

THE BUDGET OF THE UNITED NATIONS[27]

The amount of assessments paid to the United Nations is determined by the size of each nation's economy relative to the global economy as a whole. In the years immediately after World War II the US percentage of total assessments was as high as 40 percent. Today it stands at just under 25 percent, with Japan rapidly approaching at just under 20 percent.

γ γ γ

UN Assessments for Regular Budget for 2003
Total Revenues from Assessments: $1.409 billion

Country	Total Assessment for 2003	Percentage of Total Assessments
United States	$341 million	24 percent
Japan	263	19
Germany	132	9.4
France	87	6.2
United Kingdom	75	5.3
Italy	68	4.8
Canada	35	2.5
Spain	34	2.4
Brazil	32	2.3
Republic of Korea	25	1.8
Netherlands	23	1.6
Australia	22	1.6
China	21	1.5
Switzerland	17	1.2
Russia	16	1.1

27. http://www.globalpolicy.org/finance/tables/reg-budget/large03.htm

DOCUMENT NO. 28

THE BRAHIMI REPORT: REFORM OF UN PEACEKEEPING OPERATIONS[28]

This is the executive summary of a larger report on peacekeeping, also known as the Brahimi Report, after the chairman of its panel, Lakhdar Brahimi of Algeria. It called for radical reform of peacekeeping operations.

γ   γ   γ

Report of the Panel on United Nations Peacekeeping Operations

August 21, 2000

EXECUTIVE SUMMARY:

The United Nations was founded, in the words of its Charter, in order "to save succeeding generations from the scourge of war." Meeting this challenge is the most important function of the Organization, and to a very significant degree it is the yardstick with which the Organization is judged by the peoples it exists to serve. Over the last decade, the United Nations has repeatedly failed to meet the challenge, and it can do no better today. Without renewed commitment on the part of Member States, significant institutional change and increased financial support, the United Nations will not be capable of executing the critical peacekeeping and peace-building tasks that the Member States assign to it in coming months and years. There are many tasks which United Nations peacekeeping forces should not be asked to undertake and many places they should not go. But when the United Nations does send its forces to uphold the peace, they must be prepared to confront the lingering forces of war and violence, with the ability and determination to defeat them.

The Secretary-General has asked the Panel on United Nations Peace Operations, composed of individuals experienced in various aspects of conflict prevention, peacekeeping and peace-building, to assess the short-

28. http://www.un.org/peace/reports/peace_operations/

comings of the existing system and to make frank, specific and realistic recommendations for change. Our recommendations focus not only on politics and strategy but also and perhaps even more so on operational and organizational areas of need.

For preventive initiatives to succeed in reducing tension and averting conflict, the Secretary-General needs clear, strong and sustained political support from Member States. Furthermore, as the United Nations has bitterly and repeatedly discovered over the last decade, no amount of good intentions can substitute for the fundamental ability to project credible force if complex peacekeeping, in particular, is to succeed. But force alone cannot create peace; it can only create the space in which peace may be built. Moreover, the changes that the Panel recommends will have no lasting impact unless Member States summon the political will to support the United Nations politically, financially and operationally to enable the United Nations to be truly credible as a force for peace.

Each of the recommendations contained in the present report is designed to remedy a serious problem in strategic direction, decision-making, rapid deployment, operational planning and support, and the use of modern information technology. Key assessments and recommendations are highlighted below, largely in the order in which they appear in the body of the text (the numbers of the relevant paragraphs in the main text are provided in parentheses). In addition, a summary of recommendations is contained in the annex.

Experience of the past

It should have come as no surprise to anyone that some of the missions of the past decade would be particularly hard to accomplish: they tended to deploy where conflict had not resulted in victory for any side, where a military stalemate or international pressure or both had brought fighting to a halt but at least some of the parties to the conflict were not seriously committed to ending the confrontation. United Nations operations thus did not deploy into post-conflict situations but tried to create them. In such complex operations, peacekeepers work to maintain a secure local environment while peace-builders work to make that environment self-sustaining. Only such an environment offers a ready exit to peacekeeping forces, making peacekeepers and peacebuilders inseparable partners.

Implications for preventive action and peace-building: the need for strategy and support

The United Nations and its members face a pressing need to establish more effective strategies for conflict prevention, in both the long and short terms. In this context, the Panel endorses the recommendations of the Secretary-General with respect to conflict prevention contained in the Millennium Report (A/54/2000) and in his remarks before the Security Council's second open meeting on conflict prevention in July 2000. It also encourages the Secretary-General's more frequent use of fact-finding missions to areas of tension in support of short-term crisis-preventive action.

Furthermore, the Security Council and the General Assembly's Special Committee on Peacekeeping Operations, conscious that the United Nations will continue to face the prospect of having to assist communities and nations in making the transition from war to peace, have each recognized and acknowledged the key role of peace-building in complex peace operations. This will require that the United Nations system address what has hitherto been a fundamental deficiency in the way it has conceived of, funded and implemented peace-building strategies and activities. Thus, the Panel recommends that the Executive Committee on Peace and Security (ECPS) present to the Secretary-General a plan to strengthen the permanent capacity of the United Nations to develop peace-building strategies and to implement programs in support of those strategies.

Among the changes that the Panel supports are: a doctrinal shift in the use of civilian police and related rule of law elements in peace operations that emphasizes a team approach to upholding the rule of law and respect for human rights and helping communities coming out of a conflict to achieve national reconciliation; consolidation of disarmament, demobilization, and reintegration programs into the assessed budgets of complex peace operations in their first phase; flexibility for heads of United Nations peace operations to fund "quick impact projects" that make a real difference in the lives of people in the mission area; and better integration of electoral assistance into a broader strategy for the support of governance institutions.

Implications for peacekeeping: the need for robust doctrine and realistic mandates

The Panel concurs that consent of the local parties, impartiality and the use of force only in self-defense should remain the bedrock principles of peacekeeping. Experience shows, however, that in the context of intra-State/transnational conflicts, consent may be manipulated in many ways. Impartiality for United Nations operations must therefore mean adherence to the principles of the Charter: where one party to a peace agreement clearly and incontrovertibly is violating its terms, continued equal treatment of all parties by the United Nations can in the best case result in ineffectiveness and in the worst may amount to complicity with evil. No failure did more to damage the standing and credibility of United Nations peacekeeping in the 1990s than its reluctance to distinguish victim from aggressor.

In the past, the United Nations has often found itself unable to respond effectively to such challenges. It is a fundamental premise of the present report, however, that it must be able to do so. Once deployed, United Nations peacekeepers must be able to carry out their mandate professionally and successfully. This means that United Nations military units must be capable of defending themselves, other mission components and the mission's mandate. Rules of engagement should be sufficiently robust and not force United Nations contingents to cede the initiative to their attackers.

This means, in turn, that the Secretariat must not apply best-case planning assumptions to situations where the local actors have historically exhibited worst-case behavior. It means that mandates should specify an operation's authority to use force. It means bigger forces, better equipped and more costly but able to be a credible deterrent. In particular, United Nations forces for complex operations should be afforded the field intelligence and other capabilities needed to mount an effective defense against violent challengers.

Moreover, United Nations peacekeepers—troops or police—who witness violence against civilians should be presumed to be authorized to stop it, within their means, in support of basic United Nations principles. However, operations given a broad and explicit mandate for civilian protection must be given the specific resources needed to carry out that mandate.

The Secretariat must tell the Security Council what it needs to know, not what it wants to hear, when recommending force and other resource levels for a new mission, and it must set those levels according to realistic scenarios that take into account likely challenges to implementation. Security Council mandates, in turn, should reflect the clarity that peacekeeping operations require for unity of effort when they deploy into potentially dangerous situations.

The current practice is for the Secretary-General to be given a Security Council resolution specifying troop levels on paper, not knowing whether he will be given the troops and other personnel that the mission needs to function effectively, or whether they will be properly equipped. The Panel is of the view that, once realistic mission requirements have been set and agreed to, the Council should leave its authorizing resolution in draft form until the Secretary-General confirms that he has received troop and other commitments from Member States sufficient to meet those requirements.

Member States that do commit formed military units to an operation should be invited to consult with the members of the Security Council during mandate formulation; such advice might usefully be institutionalized via the establishment of ad hoc subsidiary organs of the Council, as provided for in Article 29 of the Charter. Troop contributors should also be invited to attend Secretariat briefings of the Security Council pertaining to crises that affect the safety and security of mission personnel or to a change or reinterpretation of the mandate regarding the use of force.

New headquarters capacity for information management and strategic analysis

The Panel recommends that a new information-gathering and analysis entity be created to support the informational and analytical needs of the Secretary-General and the members of the Executive Committee on Peace and Security (ECPS). Without such capacity, the Secretariat will remain a reactive institution, unable to get ahead of daily events, and the ECPS will not be able to fulfill the role for which it was created.

The Panel's proposed ECPS Information and Strategic Analysis Secretariat (EISAS) would create and maintain integrated databases on peace and security issues, distribute that knowledge efficiently within the United Nations system, generate policy analyses, formulate long-term strategies for ECPS and bring budding crises to the attention of the ECPS leadership. It could also propose and manage the agenda of ECPS itself, helping to transform it into the decision-making body anticipated in the Secretary-General's initial reforms.

The Panel proposes that EISAS be created by consolidating the existing Situation Center of the Department of Peacekeeping Operations (DPKO) with a number of small, scattered policy planning offices, and adding a small team of military analysts, experts in international criminal networks and information systems specialists. EISAS should serve the needs of all members of ECPS.

Improved mission guidance and leadership

The Panel believes it is essential to assemble the leadership of a new mission as early as possible at United Nations Headquarters, to participate in shaping a mission's concept of operations, support plan, budget, staffing and Headquarters mission guidance. To that end, the Panel recommends that the Secretary-General compile, in a systematic fashion and with input from Member States, a comprehensive list of potential special representatives of the Secretary-General (SRSGs), force commanders, civilian police commissioners, their potential deputies and potential heads of other components of a mission, representing a broad geographic and equitable gender distribution.

Rapid deployment standards and "on-call" expertise

The first 6 to 12 weeks following a ceasefire or peace accord are often the most critical ones for establishing both a stable peace and the credibility of a new operation. Opportunities lost during that period are hard to regain.

The Panel recommends that the United Nations define "rapid and effective deployment capacity" as the ability to fully deploy traditional peacekeeping operations within 30 days of the adoption of a Security Council resolution establishing such an operation, and within 90 days in the case of complex peacekeeping operations.

The Panel recommends that the United Nations standby arrangements system (UNSAS) be developed further to include several coherent, multinational, brigade-size forces and the necessary enabling forces, created by Member States working in partnership, in order to better meet the need for the robust peacekeeping forces that the Panel has advocated. The Panel also recommends that the Secretariat send a team to confirm the readiness of each potential troop contributor to meet the requisite United Nations training and equipment requirements for peacekeeping operations, prior to deployment. Units that do not meet the requirements must not be deployed.

To support such rapid and effective deployment, the Panel recommends that a revolving "on-call list" of about 100 experienced, well qualified military officers, carefully vetted and accepted by DPKO, be created within UNSAS. Teams drawn from this list and available for duty on seven days' notice would translate broad, strategic-level mission concepts developed at Headquarters into concrete operational and tactical plans in advance of the deployment of troop contingents, and would augment a core element from DPKO to serve as part of a mission start-up team.

Parallel on-call lists of civilian police, international judicial experts, penal experts and human rights specialists must be available in sufficient numbers to strengthen rule of law institutions, as needed, and should also be part of UNSAS. Pre-trained teams could then be drawn from this list to precede the main body of civilian police and related specialists into a new mission area, facilitating the rapid and effective deployment of the law and order component into the mission.

The Panel also calls upon Member States to establish enhanced national "pools" of police officers and related experts, earmarked for deployment to United Nations peace operations, to help meet the high demand for civilian police and related criminal justice/rule of law expertise in peace operations dealing with intra-State conflict. The Panel also urges Member States to consider forming joint regional partnerships and programs for the purpose of training members of the respective national pools to United Nations civilian police doctrine and standards.

The Secretariat should also address, on an urgent basis, the needs: to put in place a transparent and decentralized recruitment mechanism for civilian field personnel; to improve the retention of the civilian specialists that are needed in every complex peace operation; and to create standby arrangements for their rapid deployment.

Finally, the Panel recommends that the Secretariat radically alter the systems and procedures in place for peacekeeping procurement in order to facilitate rapid deployment. It recommends that responsibilities for peacekeeping budgeting and procurement be moved out of the Department of Management and placed in DPKO. The Panel proposes the creation of a new and distinct body of streamlined field procurement policies and procedures; increased delegation of procurement authority to the field; and greater flexibility for field missions in the management of their budgets. The Panel also urges that the Secretary-General formulate and submit to the General Assembly, for its approval, a global logistics support strategy governing the stockpiling of equipment reserves and standing contracts with the private sector for common goods and services. In the interim, the Panel recommends that additional "start-up kits" of essential equipment be maintained at the United Nations Logistics Base (UNLB) in Brindisi, Italy.

The Panel also recommends that the Secretary-General be given authority, with the approval of the Advisory Committee on Administrative and Budgetary Questions (ACABQ) to commit up to $50 million well in advance of the adoption of a Security Council resolution establishing a new operation once it becomes clear that an operation is likely to be established.

Enhance Headquarters capacity to plan and support peace operations

The Panel recommends that Headquarters support for peacekeeping be treated as a core activity of the United Nations, and as such the majority of its resource requirements should be funded through the regular budget of the Organization. DPKO and other offices that plan and support peacekeeping are currently primarily funded by the Support Account, which is renewed each year and funds only temporary posts. That approach to funding and staff seems to confuse the temporary nature of specific operations with the evident permanence of peacekeeping and other peace operations activities as core functions of the United Nations, which is obviously an untenable state of affairs.

The total cost of DPKO and related Headquarters support offices for peacekeeping does not exceed $50 million per annum, or roughly 2 per cent of total peacekeeping costs. Additional resources for those offices are urgently needed to ensure that more than $2 billion spent on peacekeeping in 2001 are well spent. The Panel therefore recommends that the Secretary-General submit a proposal to the General Assembly outlining the Organization's requirements in full.

The Panel believes that a methodical management review of DPKO should be conducted but also believes that staff shortages in certain areas are plainly obvious. For example, it is clearly not enough to have 32 officers providing military planning and guidance to 27,000 troops in the field, nine civilian police staff to identify, vet and provide guidance for up to 8,600 police, and 15 political desk officers for 14 current operations and two new ones, or to allocate just 1.25 per cent of the total costs of peacekeeping to Headquarters administrative and logistics support.

Establish Integrated Mission Task Forces for mission planning and support

The Panel recommends that Integrated Mission Task Forces (IMTFs) be created, with staff from throughout the United Nations system seconded to them, to plan new missions and help them reach full deployment, significantly enhancing the support that Headquarters provides to the field. There is currently no integrated planning or support cell in the Secretariat that brings together those responsible for political analysis, military operations, civilian police, electoral assistance, human rights, development, humanitarian assistance, refugees and displaced persons, public information, logistics, finance and recruitment.

Structural adjustments are also required in other elements of DPKO, in particular to the Military and Civilian Police Division, which should be reorganized into two separate divisions, and the Field Administration and Logistics Division (FALD), which should be split into two divisions. The Lessons Learned Unit should be strengthened and moved into the DPKO Office of Operations. Public information planning and support at Headquarters also needs strengthening, as do elements in the Department of Political Affairs (DPA), particularly the electoral unit. Outside the Secretariat, the ability of the Office of the United Nations High Commissioner for Human Rights to plan and support the human rights components of peace operations needs to be reinforced.

Consideration should be given to allocating a third Assistant Secretary-General to DPKO and designating one of them as "Principal Assistant Secretary-General", functioning as the deputy to the Under-Secretary-General.

Adapting peace operations to the information age

Modern, well utilized information technology (IT) is a key enabler of many of the above-mentioned objectives, but gaps in strategy, policy and practice impede its effective use. In particular, Headquarters lacks a sufficiently strong responsibility centre for user-level IT strategy and policy in peace operations. A senior official with such responsibility in the peace and security arena should be appointed and located within EISAS, with counterparts in the offices of the SRSG in every United Nations peace operation.

Headquarters and the field missions alike also need a substantive, global, Peace Operations Extranet (POE), through which missions would have access to, among other things, EISAS databases and analyses and lessons learned.

Challenges to implementation

The Panel believes that the above recommendations fall well within the bounds of what can be reasonably demanded of the Organization's Member States. Implementing some of them will require additional resources for the Organization, but we do not mean to suggest that the best way to solve the problems of the United Nations is merely to throw additional resources at them. Indeed, no amount of money or resources can substitute for the significant changes that are urgently needed in the culture of the Organization.

The Panel calls on the Secretariat to heed the Secretary-General's initiatives to reach out to the institutions of civil society; to constantly keep in mind that the United Nations they serve is the universal organization. People everywhere are fully entitled to consider that it is their organization, and as such to pass judgment on its activities and the people who serve in it.

Furthermore, wide disparities in staff quality exist and those in the system are the first to acknowledge it; better performers are given unreasonable workloads to compensate for those who are less capable. Unless the United Nations takes steps to become a true meritocracy, it will not be able to reverse the alarming trend of qualified personnel, the young among them in particular, leaving the Organization. Moreover, qualified people will have no incentive to join it. Unless managers at all levels, beginning with the Secretary-General and his senior staff, seriously address this problem on a priority basis, reward excellence and remove incompetence, additional resources will be wasted and lasting reform will become impossible.

Member States also acknowledge that they need to reflect on their working culture and methods. It is incumbent upon Security Council members, for example, and the membership at large to breathe life into the words that they produce, as did, for instance, the Security Council delegation that flew to Jakarta and Dili in the wake of the East Timor crisis in 1999, an example of effective Council action at its best: res, non verba.

We—the members of the Panel on United Nations Peace Operations— call on the leaders of the world assembled at the Millennium Summit, as they renew their commitment to the ideals of the United Nations, to commit as well to strengthen the capacity of the United Nations to fully accomplish the mission which is, indeed, its very raison d'être: to help communities engulfed in strife and to maintain or restore peace.

While building consensus for the recommendations in the present report, we have also come to a shared vision of a United Nations, extending a strong helping hand to a community, country or region to avert conflict or to end violence. We see an SRSG ending a mission well accomplished, having given the people of a country the opportunity to do for themselves what they could not do before: to build and hold onto peace, to find reconciliation, to strengthen democracy, to secure human rights. We see, above all, a United Nations that has not only the will but also the ability to fulfill its great promise, and to justify the confidence and trust placed in it by the overwhelming majority of humankind.

DOCUMENT NO. 29

THE UN'S REPORT ON THE MASSACRE AT SREBRENICA, BOSNIA[29]

The 1995 massacre at Srebrenica ranks, after Rwanda, among the United Nations' chief failures. This report by Secretary General Kofi Annan, excerpted here, came out in 1998, reexamining mistakes while seeking to draw lessons for future guidance.

γ   γ   γ

Report of the Secretary General (excerpted)
PURSUANT TO GENERAL ASSEMBLY RESOLUTION 53/35
November 15, 1999

The United Nations had a mandate to deter attacks on Srebrenica and five other safe areas in Bosnia and Herzegovina. Despite that mandate, up to 20,000 people, overwhelmingly from the Bosnian Muslim community, were killed in and around the safe areas. In addition, a majority of the 117 members of UNPROFOR who lost their lives in Bosnia and Herzegovina died in or around the safe areas. In requesting the submission of the present report, the General Assembly has afforded me the opportunity to explain why the United Nations failed to deter the Serb attack on Srebrenica and the appalling events that followed.

29. http://www.haverford.edu/relg/sells/reports/UNsrebrenicareport.htm

In my effort to get closer to the truth, I [Secretary General Kofi Annan] have returned to the origins of the safe area policy, discussing the evolution of that policy over a period of several years. I have drawn the attention of the reader to the resolutions of the Security Council and to the resources made available to implement those resolutions; I have reviewed how the policy was implemented on the ground, as well as the attacks that took place on other safe areas: Sarajevo, Gorazde, Bihac. I have reviewed the debate that took place within the international community on the use of force and, in particular, on the use of air power by the North Atlantic Treaty Organization (NATO). I have also reviewed the role of the United Nations Protection Force (UNPROFOR) in the fall of Srebrenica, and in the almost-forgotten case of Zepa. Finally, I recall how, having failed to act decisively during all of these events, the international community found a new will after the fall of Srebrenica and how, after the last Serb attack on the safe area of Sarajevo, a concerted military operation was launched to ensure that no such attacks would take place again.

In reviewing these events, I have in no way sought to deflect criticism directed at the United Nations Secretariat. Having served as Under-Secretary-General for Peacekeeping Operations during much of the period under review, I am fully cognizant of the mandate entrusted to the United Nations and only too painfully aware of the Organizations failures in implementing that mandate. Rather, my purpose in going over the background of the failure of the safe area policy has been to illuminate the process by which the United Nations found itself, in July 1995, confronted with these shocking events. There is an issue of responsibility, and we in the United Nations share in that responsibility, as the assessment at the end of this report records. Equally important, there are lessons to be drawn by all of those involved in the formulation and implementation of international responses to events such as the war in Bosnia and Herzegovina. There are lessons for the Secretariat, and there are lessons for the Member States that shaped the international response to the collapse of the former Yugoslavia. . . .

The Fall of Srebrenica: An Assessment

The tragedy that took place following the fall of Srebrenica is shocking for two reasons. It is shocking, first and foremost, for the magnitude of the crimes committed. Not since the horrors of World War II had Europe witnessed massacres on this scale. The mortal remains of close to 2,500 men and boys have been found on the surface, in mass grave sites and in secondary burial sites. Several thousand more men are still missing, and there is every reason to believe that additional burial sites, many of which have been probed but not exhumed, will reveal the bodies of thousands more men and boys. The great majority of those who were killed were not killed in combat: the exhumed bodies of the victims show large numbers had their hands bound, or were blindfolded, or were shot in the back or the back of the head. Numerous eyewitness accounts, now well corroborated by forensic evidence, attest to scenes of mass slaughter of unarmed victims.

The fall of Srebrenica is also shocking because the enclave's inhabitants believed that the authority of the United Nations Security Council, the presence of UNPROFOR peacekeepers, and the might of NATO air power, would ensure their safety. Instead, the Serb forces ignored the Security Council, pushed aside the UNPROFOR troops, and assessed correctly that air power would not be used to stop them. They overran the safe area of Srebrenica with ease, and then proceeded to depopulate the territory within 48 hours. Their leaders then engaged in high-level negotiations with representatives of the international community while their forces on the ground executed and buried thousands of men and boys within a matter of days.

Questions must be answered, and foremost among these are the following: how can this have been allowed to happen? And how will the United Nations ensure that no future peacekeeping operation witnesses such a calamity on its watch? In this assessment, factors ranging from the most proximate to the more over-arching will be discussed, in order to provide the most comprehensive analysis possible of the preceding narrative.

The role of UNPROFOR forces in Srebrenica:

In the effort to assign responsibility for the appalling events that took place in Srebrenica, many observers have been quick to point to the soldiers of the UNPROFOR Dutch battalion as the most immediate culprits. They blame them for not attempting to stop the Serb attack, and they blame them for not protecting the thousands of people who sought refuge in their compound.

As concerns the first criticism, the commander of the Dutch battalion believed that the Bosniacs could not defend Srebrenica by themselves and that his own forces could not be effective without substantial air support. Air support was, in his view, the most effective resource at his disposal to respond to the Serb attack. Accordingly, he requested air support on a number of occasions, even after many of his own troops had been taken hostage and faced potential Serb reprisal. These requests were unheeded by his superiors at various levels, and some of them may not have been received at all, illustrating the command-and-control problems from which UNPROFOR suffered throughout its history. However, having been told that the risk of confrontation with the Serbs was to be avoided, and that the execution of the mandate was secondary to the security of his personnel, the Dutch battalion withdrew from Observation Posts under direct attack.

It is true that the Dutch UNPROFOR troops in Srebrenica never fired at the attacking Serbs. They fired warning shots over the Serbs' heads and their mortars fired flares, but they never directly fired on any Serb units. Had they engaged the attacking Serbs directly it is possible that events would have unfolded differently. At the same time, it must be recognized that the 150 fighting men of the Dutch battalion were lightly armed and in indefensible positions, and were faced with 2,000 Serbs advancing with the support of armour and artillery.

As concerns the second criticism, it is easy to say with the benefit of hindsight and the knowledge of what followed that the Dutch battalion did not do enough to protect those who sought refuge in their compound. Perhaps they should have allowed everyone into the compound and then offered themselves as human shields to protect them. This may have slowed down the Serbs and bought time for higher level negotiations to take effect. At the same time, it is also possible that the Serb forces would then have shelled the compound, killing thousands in the process, as they had threatened to do. Ultimately, it is not possible to say with any certainty that stronger actions by the Dutch would have saved lives, and it is even possible that such efforts could have done more harm than good. Faced with this prospect and unaware that the

Serbs would proceed to execute thousands of men and boys, the Dutch avoided armed confrontation and appealed in the process for support at the highest levels.

It is harder to explain why the Dutch battalion did not report more fully the scenes that were unfolding around them following the enclave's fall. Although they did not witness mass killing, they were aware of some sinister indications. It is possible that if the members of the Dutch battalion had immediately reported in detail those sinister indications to the United Nations chain of command, the international community may have been compelled to respond more robustly and more quickly, and that some lives might have been saved. This failure of intelligence-sharing was also not limited to the fall of Srebrenica, but an endemic weakness throughout the conflict, both within the peacekeeping mission, and between the mission and Member States. . . .

The role of air power:

The next question that must be asked is this: Why was NATO air power not brought to bear upon the Serbs before they entered the town of Srebrenica? Even in the most restrictive interpretation of the mandate the use of close air support against attacking Serb targets was clearly warranted. The Serbs were firing directly at Dutch Observation Posts with tank rounds as early as 5 days before the enclave fell.

Some have alleged that NATO air power was not authorized earlier, despite repeated requests from the Dutchbat Commander, because the Force Commander or someone else had renounced its use against the Serbs in return for the release of United Nations personnel taken hostage in May–June 1995. Nothing found in the course of the preparation of this report supports such a view.

What is clear is that my predecessor, his senior advisers (amongst whom I was included as Under-Secretary-General for Peacekeeping Operations), the SRSG and the Force Commander were all deeply reluctant to use air power against the Serbs for four main reasons. We believed that by using air power against the Serbs we would be perceived as having entered the war against them, something not authorized by the Security Council and potentially fatal for a peacekeeping operation. Second, we risked losing control over the process—once the key was turned on we did not know if we would be able to turn it off', with grave consequences for the safety of the troops entrusted to us by Member States. Third, we believed that the use of air power would disrupt the primary mission of UNPROFOR as we then saw it: the creation of an environment in which the humanitarian aid could be delivered to the civilian population of the country. And fourth, we feared Serb reprisal against our peacekeepers. Member States had placed thousands of their troops under United Nations command. We, and many of the troop contributing nations, considered the security of these troops to be of fundamental importance in the implementation of the mandate. That there was merit in our concerns was evidenced by the hostage crisis of May-June 1995.

At the same time, we were fully aware that the threat of NATO air power was all we had at our disposal to respond to an attack on the safe areas. The lightly armed forces in the enclaves would be no match for (and were not intended to resist) a Serb attack supported by infantry and armour. It was thus incumbent upon us, our concerns notwithstanding, to make full use of the air power deterrent, as we had done with some effect in response to Serb attacks upon Sarajevo and Gorazde in February and April 1994, respectively. For the reasons mentioned above, we did not use with full effectiveness this one instrument at our disposal to make the safe areas at least a little bit safer. We were, with hindsight, wrong to declare repeatedly and publicly that we did not want to use air power against the Serbs except as a last resort, and to accept the shelling of the safe areas as a daily occurrence. We believed there was no choice under the Security Council resolutions but to deploy more and more peacekeepers into harm's way. The Serbs knew this, and they timed their attack on Srebrenica well. The UNPROFOR Commander in Sarajevo at the time noted that the reluctance of his superiors and of key troop contributors to escalate the use of force in the wake of the hostage crisis would create the conditions in which we would then always be stared down by the Serbs. . . .

The Role of the Security Council and Member States:

With the benefit of hindsight, one can see that many of the errors the United Nations made flowed from a single and no-doubt well-intentioned effort: we tried to keep the peace and apply the rules of peace-

keeping when there was no peace to keep. Knowing that any other course
of action would jeopardize the lives of the troops, we tried to create—or
imagine—an environment in which the tenets of peacekeeping—agreement between the parties, deployment by consent, and impartiality—
could be upheld. We tried to stabilize the situation on the ground
through ceasefire agreements, which brought us close to the Serbs, who
controlled the larger proportion of the land. We tried to eschew the use
of force except in self-defense, which brought us into conflict with the
defenders of the safe areas, whose safety depended on our use of force.

In spite of the untenability of its position, UNPROFOR was able to
assist in the humanitarian process, and to mitigate some—but, as Srebrenica tragically underscored, by no means all—the suffering inflicted
by the war. There are people alive in Bosnia today who would not be
alive had UNPROFOR not been deployed. To this extent, it can be said
that the 117 young men who lost their lives in the service of UNPRO-
FOR's mission in Bosnia and Herzegovina did not die in vain. Their
sacrifice and the good work of many others, however, cannot fully re-
deem a policy that was, at best, a half-measure.

The community of nations decided to respond to the war in Bosnia and
Herzegovina with an arms embargo, with humanitarian aid and with
the deployment of a peacekeeping force. It must be clearly stated that
these measures were poor substitutes for more decisive and forceful action to prevent the unfolding horror. The arms embargo did little more
than freeze in place the military balance within the former Yugoslavia.
It left the Serbs in a position of overwhelming military dominance and
effectively deprived the Republic of Bosnia and Herzegovina of its right,
under the Charter of the United Nations, to self-defense. It was not
necessarily a mistake to impose an arms embargo, which after all had
been done when Bosnia-Herzegovina was not yet a Member State of the
United Nations. But having done so, there must surely have been some
attendant duty to protect Bosnia and Herzegovina, after it became a
Member State, from the tragedy that then befell it. Even as the Serb
attacks on and strangulation of the safe areas continued in 1993 and
1994, all widely covered by the media and, presumably, by diplomatic
and intelligence reports to their respective governments, the approach
of the Members of the Security Council remained largely constant.

The international community still could not find the political will to confront the menace defying it.

Nor was the provision of humanitarian aid a sufficient response to ethnic cleansing and to an attempted genocide. The provision of food and shelter to people who have neither is wholly admirable, and we must all recognize the extraordinary work done by UNHCR and its partners in circumstances of extreme adversity. But the provision of humanitarian assistance could never have been a solution to the problem in that country. The problem, which cried out for a political/ military solution, was that a Member State of the United Nations, left largely defenceless as a result of an arms embargo imposed upon it by the United Nations, was being dismembered by forces committed to its destruction. This was not a problem with a humanitarian solution.

Nor was the deployment of a peacekeeping force a coherent response to this problem. My predecessor openly told the Security Council that a United Nations peacekeeping force could not bring peace to Bosnia and Herzegovina. He said it often and he said it loudly, fearing that peacekeeping techniques inevitably would fail in a situation of war. None of the conditions for the deployment of peacekeepers had been met: there was no peace agreement—not even a functioning ceasefire—there was no clear will to peace and there was no clear consent by the belligerents. Nevertheless, faute de mieux, the Security Council decided that a United Nations peacekeeping force would be deployed. Lightly armed, highly visible in their white vehicles, scattered across the country in numerous indefensible observation posts, they were able to confirm the obvious: there was no peace to keep.

In so doing, the Council obviously expected that the warring parties on the ground would respect the authority of the United Nations and would not obstruct or attack its humanitarian operations. It soon became apparent that, with the end of the Cold War and the ascendancy of irregular forces, controlled or uncontrolled, the old rules of the game no longer held. Nor was it sufficiently appreciated that a systematic and ruthless campaign such as the one conducted by the Serbs would view a United Nations humanitarian operation, not as an obstacle, but as an instrument of its aims. In such an event, it is clear that the ability to adapt mandates to the reality on the ground is of critical importance to ensuring that the appropriate force under the appropriate structure is deployed. None of that flexibility was present in the management of UNPROFOR. . . .

Lessons for the Future:

The fall of Srebrenica is replete with lessons for this Organization and its Member States—lessons that must be learned if we are to expect the peoples of the world to place their faith in the United Nations. There are occasions when Member States cannot achieve consensus on a particular response to active military conflicts, or do not have the will to pursue what many might consider to be an appropriate course of action. The first of the general lessons is that when peacekeeping operations are used as a substitute for such political consensus they will likely fail. There is a role for peacekeeping—a proud role in a world still riven by conflict—and there is even a role for protected zones and safe havens in certain situations. But peacekeeping and war fighting are distinct activities which should not be mixed. Peacekeepers must never again be deployed into an environment in which there is no ceasefire or peace agreement. Peacekeepers must never again be told that they must use their peacekeeping tools—lightly armed soldiers in scattered positions —to impose the ill-defined wishes of the international community on one or another of the belligerents by military means. If the necessary resources are not provided—and the necessary political, military and moral judgments are not made—the job simply cannot be done.

Protected zones and safe areas can have a role in protecting civilians in armed conflict. But it is clear that they either must be demilitarized and established by the agreement of the belligerents, as with the protected zones' and safe havens recognized by international humanitarian law, or they must be truly safe areas', fully defended by a credible military deterrent. The two concepts are absolutely distinct and must not be confused. It is tempting for critics to blame the UNPROFOR units in Srebrenica for its fall, or to blame the United Nations hierarchy above those units. Certainly, errors of judgment were made—errors rooted in a philosophy of impartiality and nonviolence wholly unsuited to the conflict in Bosnia—but this must not divert us from the more fundamental mistakes. The safe areas were established by the Security Council without the consent of the parties and without providing any credible military deterrent. They were neither protected areas nor "safe havens" in the sense of international humanitarian law, nor safe areas in any militarily meaningful sense. Several representatives on the Council, as well as the Secretariat, noted this problem at the time, warning that, in failing to provide a credible military deterrent, the safe area policy would be gravely damaging to the Council's reputation and, indeed, to the United Nations as a whole.

The approach by the United Nations Secretariat, the Security Council, the Contact Group and other involved Governments to the war in Bosnia and Herzegovina had certain consequences at both the political and the military level. At the political level, it entailed continuing negotiations with the architects of the Serb policies, principally, Mr. Miloseviç and Dr. Karadziç. At the military level, it resulted in a process of negotiation with and reliance upon General Mladiç, whose implacable commitment to clear Eastern Bosnia, and Sarajevo if possible, of Bosniacs was plainly obvious and led inexorably to Srebrenica. At various points during the war, these negotiations amounted to appeasement.

The international community as a whole must accept its share of responsibility for allowing this tragic course of events by its prolonged refusal to use force in the early stages of the war. This responsibility is shared by the Security Council, the Contact Group and other Governments which contributed to the delay in the use of force, as well as by the United Nations Secretariat and the Mission in the field. But clearly the primary and most direct responsibility lies with the architects and implementers of the attempted genocide in Bosnia. Radovan Karadziç and Ratko Mladiç, along with their major collaborators, have been indicted by the International Criminal Tribunal for the Former Yugoslavia. To this day, they remain free men. They must be made to answer for the barbaric crimes with which they have been charged.

The cardinal lesson of Srebrenica is that a deliberate and systematic attempt to terrorize, expel or murder an entire people must be met decisively with all necessary means, and with the political will to carry the policy through to its logical conclusion. In the Balkans, in this decade, this lesson has had to be learned not once, but twice. In both instances, in Bosnia and in Kosovo, the international community tried to reach a negotiated settlement with an unscrupulous and murderous regime. In both instances it required the use of force to bring a halt to the planned and systematic killing and expulsion of civilians.

The United Nations experience in Bosnia was one of the most difficult and painful in our history. It is with the deepest regret and remorse that we have reviewed our own actions and decisions in the face of the assault on Srebrenica. Through error, misjudgment and an inability to recognize the scope of the evil confronting us, we failed to do our part to help save the people of Srebrenica from the Serb campaign of mass murder. No one regrets more than we the opportunities for achieving peace and justice that were missed. No one laments more than we the failure of the international community to take decisive action to halt the suffering and end a war that had produced so many victims. Srebrenica crystallized a truth understood only too late by the United Nations and the world at large: that Bosnia was as much a moral cause as a military conflict. The tragedy of Srebrenica will haunt our history forever.

In the end, the only meaningful and lasting amends we can make to the citizens of Bosnia and Herzegovina who put their faith in the international community is to do our utmost not to allow such horrors to recur. When the international community makes a solemn promise to safeguard and protect innocent civilians from massacre, then it must be willing to back its promise with the necessary means. Otherwise, it is surely better not to raise hopes and expectations in the first place, and not to impede whatever capability they may be able to muster in their own defense.

To ensure that we have fully learned the lessons of the tragic history detailed in this report, I wish to encourage Member States to engage in a process of reflection and analysis, focused on the key challenges the narrative uncovers. The aim of this process would be to clarify and to improve the capacity of the United Nations to respond to various forms of conflict. I have in mind addressing such issues as the gulf between mandate and means; the inadequacy of symbolic deterrence in the face of a systematic campaign of violence; the pervasive ambivalence within the United Nations regarding the role of force in the pursuit of peace; an institutional ideology of impartiality even when confronted with attempted genocide; and a range of doctrinal and institutional issues that go to the heart of the United Nations' ability to keep the peace and help protect civilian populations from armed conflict. The Secretariat is ready to join in such a process.

The body of this report sets out in meticulous, systematic, exhaustive and ultimately harrowing detail the descent of Srebrenica into a horror without parallel in the history of Europe since the Second World War. I urge all concerned to study this report carefully, and to let the facts speak for themselves. The men who have been charged with this crime against humanity reminded the world, and, in particular, the United Nations, that evil exists in the world. They taught us also that the United Nations' global commitment to ending conflict does not preclude moral judgments, but makes them necessary. It is in this spirit that I submit my report of the fall of Srebrenica to the General Assembly, and to the world.

DOCUMENT NO. 30

PREAMBLE OF THE UNIVERSAL DECLARATION OF HUMAN RIGHTS[30]

The Charter of the United Nations mentions human rights seven times, and the promotion of human rights remains a cornerstone of the organization. The General Assembly adopted the Universal Declaration of Human Rights on December 10, 1948, the preamble of which appears in the following pages. The Declaration has been adopted by all nations of the world and the international community has declared the universality of the rights of all peoples. Its actual application has been much more problematic.

γ   γ   γ

Adopted and proclaimed by General Assembly Resolution 217 A (III)
December 10, 1948

PREAMBLE

Whereas recognition of the inherent dignity and of the equal and inalienable rights of all members of the human family is the foundation of freedom, justice and peace in the world,

30. *Yearbook of the United Nations, 1948–49* (Lake Success, NY: United Nations Office of Public Information, 1950), 535–537.

Whereas disregard and contempt for human rights have resulted in barbarous acts which have outraged the conscience of mankind, and the advent of a world in which human beings shall enjoy freedom of speech and belief and freedom from fear and want has been proclaimed as the highest aspiration of the common people,

Whereas it is essential, if man is not to be compelled to have recourse, as a last resort, to rebellion against tyranny and oppression, that human rights should be protected by the rule of law,

Whereas it is essential to promote the development of friendly relations between nations,

Whereas the peoples of the United Nations have in the Charter reaffirmed their faith in fundamental human rights, in the dignity and worth of the human person and in the equal rights of men and women and have determined to promote social progress and better standards of life in larger freedom,

Whereas Member States have pledged themselves to achieve, in cooperation with the United Nations, the promotion of universal respect for and observance of human rights and fundamental freedoms,

Whereas a common understanding of these rights and freedoms is of the greatest importance for the full realization of this pledge,

Now, Therefore THE GENERAL ASSEMBLY proclaims THIS UNIVERSAL DECLARATION OF HUMAN RIGHTS as a common standard of achievement for all peoples and all nations, to the end that every individual and every organ of society, keeping this Declaration constantly in mind, shall strive by teaching and education to promote respect for these rights and freedoms and by progressive measures, national and international, to secure their universal and effective recognition and observance, both among the peoples of Member States themselves and among the peoples of territories under their jurisdiction.

DOCUMENT NO. 31

THE UNITED NATIONS PROPOSES ACTIONS AGAINST THE TALIBAN AND AL-QUEDA IN AFGHANISTAN, 1999[31]

Two years prior to the events of 9/11 this Security Council Resolution imposed sanctions against the Taliban regime in Afghanistan, called for the closure of terrorist training camps, and demanded surrender of Al Queda leader Osama bin Laden. A subsequent Resolution, 1333, passed by the Security Council on December 19, 2000, sought to reaffirm Resolution 1267.

γ   γ   γ

UN Security Council Resolution 1267

October 15, 1999

The Security Council,

Reaffirming its previous resolutions, in particular resolutions 1189 (1998) of 13 August 1998, 1193 (1998) of 28 August 1998 and 1214 (1998) of 8 December 1998, and the statements of its President on the situation in Afghanistan,

Reaffirming its strong commitment to the sovereignty, independence, territorial integrity and national unity of Afghanistan, and its respect for Afghanistan's cultural and historical heritage,

Reiterating its deep concern over the continuing violations of international humanitarian law and of human rights, particularly discrimination against women and girls, and over the significant rise in the illicit production of opium, and stressing that the capture by the Taliban of the Consulate-General of the Islamic Republic of Iran and the murder of Iranian diplomats and a journalist in Mazar-e-Sharif constituted flagrant violations of established international law,

31. This Resolution can be obtained at the UN website at http://www.un.int/usa/sres1267.htm

Recalling the relevant international counter-terrorism conventions and in particular the obligations of parties to those conventions to extradite or prosecute terrorists,

Strongly condemning the continuing use of Afghan territory, especially areas controlled by the Taliban, for the sheltering and training of terrorists and planning of terrorist acts, and reaffirming its conviction that the suppression of international terrorism is essential for the maintenance of international peace and security,

Deploring the fact that the Taliban continues to provide safe haven to Usama bin Laden and to allow him and others associated with him to operate a network of terrorist training camps from Taliban-controlled territory and to use Afghanistan as a base from which to sponsor international terrorist operations,

Noting the indictment of Usama bin Laden and his associates by the United States of America for, inter alia, the 7 August 1998 bombings of the United States embassies in Nairobi, Kenya, and Dar es Salaam, Tanzania and for conspiring to kill American nationals outside the United States, and noting also the request of the United States of America to the Taliban to surrender them for trial (S/1999/1021),

Determining that the failure of the Taliban authorities to respond to the demands in paragraph 13 of resolution 1214 (1998) constitutes a threat to international peace and security,

Stressing its determination to ensure respect for its resolutions,

Acting under Chapter VII of the Charter of the United Nations,

1. Insists that the Afghan faction known as the Taliban, which also calls itself the Islamic Emirate of Afghanistan, comply promptly with its previous resolutions and in particular cease the provision of sanctuary and training for international terrorists and their organizations, take appropriate effective measures to ensure that the territory under its control is not used for terrorist installations and camps, or for the preparation or organization of terrorist acts against other States or their citizens, and cooperate with efforts to bring indicted terrorists to justice;

2. Demands that the Taliban turn over Usama bin Laden without further delay to appropriate authorities in a country where he has been indicted, or to appropriate authorities in a country where he will be returned to such a country, or to appropriate authorities in a country where he will be arrested and effectively brought to justice;

3. Decides that on 14 November 1999 all States shall impose the measures set out in paragraph 4 below, unless the Council has previously decided, on the basis of a report of the Secretary-General, that the Taliban has fully complied with the obligation set out in paragraph 2 above;

4. Decides further that, in order to enforce paragraph 2 above, all States shall:

(a) Deny permission for any aircraft to take off from or land in their territory if it is owned, leased or operated by or on behalf of the Taliban as designated by the Committee established by paragraph 6 below, unless the particular flight has been approved in advance by the Committee on the grounds of humanitarian need, including religious obligation such as the performance of the Hajj;

(b) Freeze funds and other financial resources, including funds derived or generated from property owned or controlled directly or indirectly by the Taliban, or by any undertaking owned or controlled by the Taliban, as designated by the Committee established by paragraph 6 below, and ensure that neither they nor any other funds or financial resources so designated are made available, by their nationals or by any persons within their territory, to or for the benefit of the Taliban or any undertaking owned or controlled, directly or indirectly, by the Taliban, except as may be authorized by the Committee on a case-by-case basis on the grounds of humanitarian need;

5. Urges all States to cooperate with efforts to fulfill the demand in paragraph 2 above, and to consider further measures against Usama bin Laden and his associates;

6. Decides to establish, in accordance with rule 28 of its provisional rules of procedure, a Committee of the Security Council consisting of

all the members of the Council to undertake the following tasks and to report on its work to the Council with its observations and recommendations:

(a) To seek from all States further information regarding the action taken by them with a view to effectively implementing the measures imposed by paragraph 4 above;

(b) To consider information brought to its attention by States concerning violations of the measures imposed by paragraph 4 above and to recommend appropriate measures in response thereto;

(c) To make periodic reports to the Council on the impact, including the humanitarian implications, of the measures imposed by paragraph 4 above;

(d) To make periodic reports to the Council on information submitted to it regarding alleged violations of the measures imposed by paragraph 4 above, identifying where possible persons or entities reported to be engaged in such violations;

(e) To designate the aircraft and funds or other financial resources referred to in paragraph 4 above in order to facilitate the implementation of the measures imposed by that paragraph;

(f) To consider requests for exemptions from the measures imposed by paragraph 4 above as provided in that paragraph, and to decide on the granting of an exemption to these measures in respect of the payment by the International Air Transport Association (IATA) to the aeronautical authority of Afghanistan on behalf of international airlines for air traffic control services;

(g) To examine the reports submitted pursuant to paragraph 9 below;

7. Calls upon all States to act strictly in accordance with the provisions of this resolution, notwithstanding the existence of any rights or obligations conferred or imposed by any international agreement or any contract entered into or any license or permit granted prior to the date of coming into force of the measures imposed by paragraph 4 above;

8. Calls upon States to bring proceedings against persons and entities within their jurisdiction that violate the measures imposed by paragraph 4 above and to impose appropriate penalties;

9. Calls upon all States to cooperate fully with the Committee established by paragraph 6 above in the fulfillment of its tasks, including supplying such information as may be required by the Committee in pursuance of this resolution;

10. Requests all States to report to the Committee established by paragraph 6 above within 30 days of the coming into force of the measures imposed by paragraph 4 above on the steps they have taken with a view to effectively implementing paragraph 4 above;

11. Requests the Secretary-General to provide all necessary assistance to the Committee established by paragraph 6 above and to make the necessary arrangements in the Secretariat for this purpose;

12. Requests the Committee established by paragraph 6 above to determine appropriate arrangements, on the basis of recommendations of the Secretariat, with competent international organizations, neighboring and other States, and parties concerned with a view to improving the monitoring of the implementation of the measures imposed by paragraph 4 above;

13. Requests the Secretariat to submit for consideration by the Committee established by paragraph 6 above information received from Governments and public sources on possible violations of the measures imposed by paragraph 4 above;

14. Decides to terminate the measures imposed by paragraph 4 above once the Secretary-General reports to the Security Council that the Taliban has fulfilled the obligation set out in paragraph 2 above;

15. Expresses its readiness to consider the imposition of further measures, in accordance with its responsibility under the Charter of the United Nations, with the aim of achieving the full implementation of this resolution;

16. Decides to remain actively seized of the matter.

BIBLIOGRAPHY

Alger, Chadwick F., ed. *The Future of the United Nations System: Potential for the Twenty-First Century.* (Tokyo: United Nations University Press, 1998).

Bailey, Sydney D., and Daws, Sam. *The Procedure of the UN Security Council.* (3rd. ed.). (Oxford: Oxford University Press, 1998).

Barnett, Michael. *Eyewitness to a Genocide: The United Nations in Rwanda.* (Ithaca, NY: Cornell University Press, 2002).

Bennett, A. LeRoy, and Oliver, James. *International Organizations: Principles and Issues.* (Upper Saddle River, NJ: Pearson Higher Education, 2002).

Boutros-Ghali, Boutros. *Unvanquished: A U.S.-U.N. Saga.* (New York: Random House, 1999).

Brown, Archie. *The Gorbachev Factor.* (Oxford: Oxford University Press, 1996).

Cumings, Bruce. *Korea's Place in the Sun: A Modern History.* (New York: W. W. Norton, 1998).

Diehl, Paul F. *International Peacekeeping.* (Baltimore: Johns Hopkins University Press, 1994).

Divine, Robert A. *Second Chance: The Triumph of Internationalism in America During World War II.* (New York: Atheneum, 1967).

Dodge, Toby. *Inventing Iraq: The Failure of Nation Building and a History Denied.* (New York: Columbia University Press, 2003).

Evans, Gareth. "Preventive Action and Conflict Resolution," in *Peacemaking and Peacekeeping for the New Century*. Otunnu, Olara et al. eds. (Oxford: Rowman and Littlefield, 1998).

Fawcett, Louise, and Hurrell, Andrew, eds. *Regionalism in World Politics: Regional Organization and International Order.* (Oxford: Oxford University Press, 1995).

Fisk, Robert. *Pity the Nation: The Abduction of Lebanon.* (Oxford: Oxford University Press, 1991).

Foot, Rosemary, et al. *US Hegemony and International Organizations.* (Oxford: Oxford University Press, 2003).

Fromkin, David. *A Peace to End All Peace: The Fall of the Ottoman Empire and the Creation of the Modern Middle East.* (New York: Henry Holt, 1989).

Gorman, Robert. *Great Debates at the United Nations: An Encyclopedia of Fifty Key Issues, 1945–2000.* (Westport, CT: Greenwood Press, 2001).

Gregg, Robert W. *About Face? The United States and the United Nations.* (London: Rienner Publishers, 1993).

Heymann, Philip. *Terrorism, Freedom, and Security.* (Cambridge, MA: MIT Press, 2003).

Hilderbrand, Robert. *Dumbarton Oaks: The Origins of the United Nations and the Search for Postwar Security.* (Chapel Hill: University of North Carolina Press, 1990).

Hiro, Dilip. *Iraq: In the Eye of the Storm.* (New York: Nation Books, 2002).

Hochschild, Adam. *King Leopold's Ghost: A Story of Greed, Terror, and Heroism in Colonial Africa.* (New York: Houghton Mifflin, 1998).

Hyland, William. *Clinton's World: Remaking American Foreign Policy.* (London: Praeger, 1999).

Keay, John. *Sowing the Wind: The Seeds of Conflict in the Middle East.* (New York: W. W. Norton, 2003).

Luard, Evan. *The United Nations: How It Works and What It Does.* (London: Macmillan, 1994).

Luck, Edward C. *Mixed Messages: American Politics and International Organization, 1919–1999.* (Washington, D.C.: Brookings Institution Press, 1999).

MacQueen, Norrie. *The United Nations Since 1945: Peacekeeping and the Cold War.* (New York: Longman, 1999).

MacQueen, Norrie. *United Nations Peacekeeping in Africa Since 1960.* (New York: Longman, 2002).

Mamdani, Mahmood. *When Victims Become Killers: Colonialism, Nativism, and the Genocide in Rwanda.* (Princeton, NJ: Princeton University Press, 2001).

Mays, Terry. *Historical Dictionary of Multinational Peacekeeping.* (London: Scarecrow Press, 1996).

Mazuzan, George. *Warren R. Austin at the U.N.: 1946–1953.* (Kent, OH: Kent State University Press, 1977).

Meisler, Stanley. *The United Nations: The First Fifty Years.* (New York: Atlantic Monthly Press, 1995).

Mingst, Karen, and Karns, Margaret P. *The United Nations in the Post-Cold War Era.* (Oxford: Westview Press, 2000).

Minter, William. *Apartheid's Contras: An Inquiry into the Roots of War in Angola and Mozambique.* (London: Zed Books, 1994).

Moore, John Allphin, and Pubantz, Jerry. *Encyclopedia of the United Nations.* (New York: Facts on File, 2002).

Moore, John Allphin, and Pubantz, Jerry. *To Create a New World: American Presidents and the United Nations.* (New York: Peter Lang Publishing, 1999).

Notter, Harley. *Postwar Foreign Policy Preparation, 1939–1945.* (Washington: U.S. Department of State, 1949).

Nzongola-Ntalaja, George *The Congo: From Leopold to Kabila.* (London: Zed Books, 2002).

Otunnu, Olara A., and Doyle, Michael W., eds. *Peacemaking and Peacekeeping for the New Century.* (New York: Rowman and Littlefield, 1998).

Paris, Timothy. *Britain, the Hashemites, and Arab Rule, 1920–1925.* (London: Frank Cass, 2003).

Ramsbotham, Tom, and Woodhouse, Oliver. *Encyclopedia of International Peace-keeping Operations.* (Santa Barbara: ABC-CLIO, 1999).

Russell, Ruth B. *A History of the United Nations Charter: The Role of the United States, 1940–1945.* (Washington, D.C.: Brookings Institution, 1958).

Ryan, Stephen. *The United Nations and International Politics.* (New York: St. Martin's Press, 2000).

Schlesinger, Stephen. *Act of Creation: The Founding of the United Nations.* (Oxford: Westview Press, 2003).

Segev, Tom. *One Palestine, Complete: Jews and Arabs Under the British Mandate.* (New York: Henry Holt, 1999).

Sen, Amartya. *Development as Freedom.* (New York: Alfred A. Knopf, 1999).

Shlaim, Avi. *The Iron Wall: Israel and the Arab World.* (New York: W. W. Norton, 2000).

Stiglitz, Joseph. *Globalization and Its Discontents.* (New York: W. W. Norton, 2002).

Stueck, William. *The Korean War: An International History.* (Princeton, NJ: Princeton University Press, 1995).

Stueck, William. *Rethinking the Korean War: A New Diplomatic and Strategic History.* (Princeton, NJ: Princeton University Press, 2002).

Taylor, Paul. *International Organization in the Age of Globalization.* (London: Continuum, 2003).

Tripp, Charles. *A History of Iraq.* (Cambridge: Cambridge University Press, 2000).

Urquhart, Brian. *Hammarskjöld.* (New York: Harper, 1972).

Weiss, Thomas; Forsythe, David; Coate, Roger. *The United Nations and Changing World Politics.* (Oxford: Westview Press, 2001).

Ziring, Lawrence, et al. *The United Nations: International Organization and World Politics.* (Orlando, FL: Harcourt College Publishers, 2000).

INDEX

ABOUT THE AUTHOR

Christopher D. O'Sullivan is the author of *Sumner Welles, Postwar Planning, and the Quest for a New World Order, 1937–1943* (Columbia University Press, 2003) which won the American Historical Association's Gutenberg-e Prize. He is currently a Fellow at the Centre for International Studies at the London School of Economics and a Fulbright Professor of International Relations and History at the University of Jordan in Amman.